WORKING FOR THE FUTURE

A TEACHER'S GUIDE

BY

GAY SEIDMAN
AND
JANET STUART

INTERNATIONAL FOUNDATION FOR EDUCATION WITH PRODUCTION
Gaborone   1990

First Published July 1990

Published by The International Foundation for Education with Production, P O Box 20906 Gaborone, Botswana

ISBN 99912-0-024-X

Printed by: Mmegi wa Dikgang Printers, P O Box 199, Serowe, Botswana
Typesetting by: Gaogakwe Tlhaloganyang, IFEP Graphics Department P O Box 20906, Gaborone, Botswana

CONTENTS

SECTION I

SECTION II

SECTION III

Class Activities by Chapters of the Textbook:

SECTION IV

SECTION I

TEACHING A CONCEPT - BASED COURSE

INTRODUCTION

The Development Studies syllalbus lays down the main aims of the course, and spells out its content objectives. I am here concerned with the **instructional objectives**, namely:

-**what kinds of knowledge and skills** do we want the students to have at the end of the course? and

-**what kinds of teaching and learning** are most likely to achieve this?

I suggest we want the students to acquire the following kinds of knowledge:

> a) a number of general **concepts** they can use to categorise information from their environment, and to organise such information in useful ways, and

> b) a number of general ideas - **generalisations** - about development, to help them understand relationships, explain cause and effect, and predict likely consequences.

Further, I suggest that the teaching-learning process wich will be most effective is one where:

> a) the role of the teacher is to **structure and guide** the learning experience of the students, giving information where needed, then teaching the students how to use it and

> b) the role of the students is to become **involved** in doing their **own** learning, under the teacher's guidance.

In Paolo Freire's terms, this is close to the "dialogic" approach, and far from the "banking" approach to teaching.

I will now try to show what I mean in practice.

1

CONCEPTS

Concepts are tools for thinking about the world. They are abstractions that enable us to discuss events and ideas in general terms, without having to refer to examples all the time. Thus, using the general concept "industry" enables us to bring together, for example, different kinds of factories, workshops and activities for making goods, and permits us to discuss how, in general, this helps development.

However, we cannot discuss "industry" unless we all know what we mean by this word. We must all have in our minds some image of groups of people working, mostly in buildings, using machinery, with some kind of power source, to produce things in large quantities. We must be sure that we are not visualising, for example, women weeding in a field.

A concept like "industry" is fairly abstract. It means little until we connect it to real objects, people or situations. Only when we have a very clear picture of what it involves in reality do we "understand" a concept. Only when we have this "understanding" can we make sensible general statements about it, such as:

-       "Industries are usually found in towns;"

-       "Industries give many people wage-employment;" and

-       "Industries need capital to get started;"

As we shall see presently, such statements are useful "generalisations". You will notice that the last two statements use other concepts, "wage-employment" and "capital".

How do we learn to undestand such concepts? How did you acquire the concept of "industry"? Gradually, or all at once? By visiting factories? Or working in one? By seeing pictures? By reading? By listening to someone who has experienced industrial work describing it? Or from several of these?

Grasping concepts in the classroom

When we teach Development Studies in schools, we want students to gain real understanding as quickly and accurately as possible. We can only do this by building on the experiences they have already had. The concept must be related to something they already know. If the concept is very far from their experience, the teacher must bridge the gap in some way so as to lead them to it.

This is often quite difficult in a classroom. But fortunately Development Studies is about the real world, and it is often possible, using a little imagination, to anchor new concepts firmly in their previous experience. If not, the teacher must provide some new "experience", either real, simulated, or of a symbolic kind, such as books and pictures.

Some possible practical ways of doing this for "industry" are listed below:

1. Arrange a visit to a factory or industrial estate.

2. Use pictures from books, magazines or newspapers, or any other form of visual aid.

3. Relate the concept of "industry" to anything in the children's environment that exemplifies it. This is easier in towns, but even rural children may have seen heavy machinery in the fields or on the roads, or building dams, or visited a large-scale workshop.

4. Use a story in an "industrial" setting, either from a book, or told dramatically by the teacher, or by an industrial worker.

The more examples used the better! Pupils may need many examples before they grasp fully what "industry" is, and what it isn't.

It is easier, of course, to do this with some concepts than others; it depends on the level of abstraciton. "Wage-employment" is easily exemplified, but "capital" is more difficult. For the latter, the teacher may need to provide a real or simulated experience: a classroom game with play-money would be a simulation, or a real productive exercise can be carried out, such as buying a box of fruit, for resale at a profit, or raising chickens. (This is where co-operative projects feed into the theoretical lessons.)

What we have discussed here is the so-called inductive approach. It is considered to lead to much better understanding of broad concepts, because it is based on the concrete experience of the students.

The relationship between facts and concepts

Concepts are probably more important than facts, but a factual base is needed as the starting point from which to develop concepts and the related generalisations.

Taking the example of "industrialisation" - a concept derived from "industry" but on a still more abstract level - we can build it up by studying factually the different kinds of productive processes in the past and the present, and by looking at what is happening in the students' own country today. Facts such as "x% of our population are miners, y% are factory workers and z% are farmers" are not themselves worth memorising - they will have changed in five years time. But they are useful because they allow students to compare their country against other countries with different proportions, so that they can call one country "industrialised" and the other "agricultural".

Only when they have reached that stage can studenets go further, to study how a country can move from being agricultural to being industrialised. At this next stage, facts will again be studied as a basis: some historical facts about the industrial revolutions in the UK and USSR; some facts about China's policies since 1949, and so forth. Again, these facts are important only because they enable the students to form generalisations such as "Industrialisation requires many workers to leave the countryside and move to towns."

The relationship between facts, concepts and generalisations

By "generalisation" I mean broad statements which express some important idea; they may describe a general state of affairs, or point to a general relationship, such as cause and effect. They usually involve the use of concepts.

4

Like concepts, generalisations can be formed at many different levels of abstraction and generality. Some merely describe, others go further. Here are some examples:

-   "Our industries are based on our mines" generalises wthin a country, while

-   "Industries are usually found in towns" generalises across the world.

Both of these are fairly concrete generalisations. A more abstract statement might be:

-   "Industrialisation implies urbanisation;"

Some generalisations give explanations. Here is one:

-   "A reason for the rapid growth of British industry in the 18th century was the capital accumulated from colonial trade."

This could be extended so that it takes the form of a more general "law of development," such as:

-   "Industrialisation requires previous capital accumulation."

It is obvious that students would not "understand" such a statement unless they had studied the facts on which it is based; it should be equally obvious that learning facts without drawing them together into such powerful and useful generalisations is often a waste of time.

Another use of facts is to check generalisations against them. Some generalisations may be in the form of a hypotheses or prediction:

-   "If a country has a good mineral resource base, industrialisation will take place."

Such a statement can - and should - then be tested out against historical and modern evidence: do all countries with good mineral resources develop industries? If not, what conditions hinder or facilitate such developments? Here, accurate facts are very important.

The relationship can be summarised in a diagram:

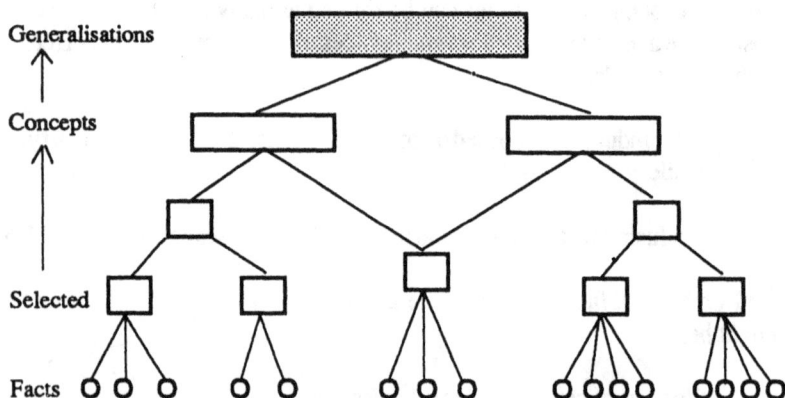

Figure 1

Summary

It is the generalisations, together with the concepts embodied in them, which Development Studies students should understand and remember. The individual facts - GNP, % of work forces, names of industries - can be forgotten once they have served their purpose. The understanding, of "industrialisation", for example, is what matters.

As far as possible, the emphasis in the exam will be on this type of understanding, rather than on testing recall of facts.

One should add, though, that understanding concepts and generalisations will help students to remember facts, which can then be used to illustrate and support the generalisations under discussion. This is, in pure academic terms, the best result of all.

TEACHING STRATEGIES

Let me spell out how the teacher can teach the syllabus in such a way. First, the teacher must have an overall view of the structure of the syllabus, and indeed, of the whole subject-matter of Development Studies. She will know what concepts and generalisations the students are to aim at, and how they can reach them. (She will also know what concepts they will probably not acquire until they are older, or go on to further study, but which depend critically on the groundwork laid in COSC.)

Secondly, the teacher needs a clear understanding of the stage students have reached, so she can build on their present experience, extending it to form the foundation for the next stage.

Thirdly, she must encourage the students to be active in their learning. In sum, the teacher has to plan the route carefully from where the students are to where she hopes they will get to. She must plan it stage by stage, paying attention to the **building up** and to the **pacing** of each part, as well as to ways students **participate** in learning. This is what constitutes the art and craft of the teacher. No matter what excellent textbooks are available, the teacher still bears responsibility for the strategy in the classroom.

Building Up

As we have said, the teacher starts with the students' own present knowledge, with their familiar environment. She starts with facts, low-level concepts, and concrete ideas and statements, easily illustrated; she builds up to broader concepts and more abstract generalisations, covering wider perspectives, until she has led the students to a peak of understanding from which they can survey all the concepts and their relationships, laid out like a map before them. (Again, perhaps this is too ambitious for COSC, but at least the teacher should take them to a peak half-way up, whence they get a clear if partial view of the subject!)

But the paths of the students and of the teacher are different in this respect: the teacher has been there before and knows the way. In fact, in planning her teaching, she works downwards: she starts with the most abstract concepts and the broadest generalisations that she hopes the students will eventually reach, and moves downwards, deciding which concepts they will need on the way, and which generalisations will make good half-way steps. Then she chooses a selection of suitable facts to study which will illustrate the ideas, and takes examples from the familiar environment to exemplify the concepts. Finally she plans the learning activities which will introduce the students to the concepts and ideas.

The students start off at the bottom: they experience the learning activities, they meet the facts, form the concepts, begin to draw suitable conclusions and make general statements. Thus gradually, through the course, they struggle upwards through a long series of ever more abstract concepts and generalisations, till they achieve the comprehension of the broad concept. Finally they understand where the teacher was taking them.

It is often a good idea to give the students a rough outline of the ground they will cover, showing them where they will be going. But they cannot start their learning at the top: they always need to climb the pathway themselves.

Figure 2 illustrates the process for "industrialisation".

Pacing

This is very important. The teacher has to ensure that each stage is assimilated before students go on to the next stage.

a)   **Internalising new knowledge.** Starting from a familiar example, or from some real or simulated experience, she will add new facts, introduce new concepts, or give a new, more technical name to some familiar phenomenon. Then she must ensure the students have taken in (assimilated) this new knowledge, and, if necessary, re-organise (accommodate) their old knowledge to fit it. For example, vague knowledge about car factories and gold mines, together with odd memories of James Watt's steam engine, might now be re-organised and fitted together as examples of "industrial processes".

This is an absolutely crucial stage. The process of internalising knowledge takes place in the students, not in the teacher. But she has to help this process. She must pause, and give time to the students to carry it out. She can organise various classroom activities to help them, for example:

-        answering structured questions orally or in writing;

8

Figure 2 Teaching "Industrialisation"

ABSTRACT CONCEPT	**HIGH-LEVEL GENERALISATION**
Industrialisation	"Industrialisation requires previous
Urbanisation	capital accumulation"
Accumulation etc.	"Urbanisation leads to a more complex
	society with a more highly differenti
	ated division of labour etc.

CONCRETE CONCEPTS	**LOW-LEVEL GENERALISATION**
Industry	"Industries are usually found in towns"
Capital	"Industries provide wage employment"
Specialisation etc.	"Workers in modern industry become
	highly specialised etc.

FACTUAL CONTENT
- Studies of currently developing countries i.e. China, Kenya, Tanza
  nia, South Africa;
- Historical accounts of industrial revolutions in UK, USSR;
- Studies of own country; statistical data; maps; plans
- Information about particular local industries

LEARNING ACTIVITIES

Reading stories and textbook	Studying tables of data
Referring to newspapers,	Visiting factories
government publications	Watching films, slides etc.
Listening to teacher or other	
expert	
Carrying out productive	
co-operative projects	

PUPILS' PREVIOUS EXPERIENCE

Earlier school knowledge   Work experience(?)
Knowledge of own community and country
Facts picked up from other sources

(*Note*: Obviously, this is not a complete list of concepts and generalisations that can be
learnt under this topic. They are a few examples to show how one can think about and plan
for concept-based learning.)

P
U
P
I
L
S

P
A
T
H
W
A
Y

Chil
start:
learnii
here

9

-   small group discussions where peers help each other to understand;

-   individual written summaries; and

-   whole class discussions.

b)   **Applying new knowledge.** The teacher must then check to see how far the students have really internalised the new knowledge and made it their own, how far they "understand" it. The only real proof of understanding is whether they can apply it: by producing it in a new form, such as a statement in their own words, a new pictorial or diagrammatic representation; by giving a new example, or by applying it to a new context. For example the question, "if we had industries in our village, what difference would it make?" tests understanding of the concept of industrialisation.

Time spent on this is well worthwhile: if basic concepts and ideas are well understood, the students will then more rapidly assimilate the next stage.

Participation in learning: doing it themselves

The teacher should encourage the students to become active partners in the learning process. Having presented them with suitable factual content, and directed their attention to relevant experiences and examples, she shoud make them draw their own conclusions, and encourage them to formulate their own generalisations at each stage.

The students may draw different conclusions from the ones the teacher had first in mind; this is all to the good. Teacher and students can together test these against the evidence. If the students have made reasonable statements, the teacher should accept these, and then encourage them to look still further.

We may consider two problems here: language and time.

a)   **Language:** Students may not use precise language at first; they may not even know the right words. Yet they may be showing understanding in spite of this. They can be guided gradually to use the correct words and concepts. To express their own ideas is the first and most important step.

10

b)   **Time:** It may seem to take much longer if we allow students to stumble around trying to formulate their own conclusions. But this is only in the early stages. When students come to realise that these efforts are important and prized by the teacher, they will improve, and with practice become much faster. Later sections of the course will be handled much more quickly and competently.

The importance of such participation cannot be over-emphasised. Firstly the students are learning to *think for themselves;* they will no longer expect the teacher to provide an answer which they can write down and memorise without understanding. They will become used to thinking out the conclusions by themselves. To learn this *process* of thinking is just as important as learning the right conclusions, if not more so.

Secondly, students will both *understand and remember* the generalisations better if they have worked their own way towards them. If they do forget a generalisation, they may even be able to work it out again for themselves!

Thirdly, when they have made the knowledge their own in this way, they will be in a position *to use* it, as specified in the general aims of the Development Studies syllabus.

There are several ways of organising the classroom to achieve these ends, but they all involve some form of *communication.* Small group discussions, class debates, making reports, writing one's own summary - all these activities force the students to rephrase and recode their knowledge, either for themselves or for others. It is in this way we make knowledge our own; in other words, it is through communicating that we learn to understand. Don't we know, as teachers, that often the first time we truly understand a topic is when we have had to teach it? Let the students experience the same thing!

THE SPIRAL CURRICULUM

It is most unlikely that pupils will grasp the full implications of an important concept or abstract generalisation in one lesson, or even after one term. The teacher needs to keep referring to it from time to time in as many different contexts as possible.

To encourage this, the Development Studies syllabus is constructed like a spiral. Students will keep meeting the most important concepts again and again, in new and more abstract forms. For example, "industrialisation", will appear in different countries (the students' own and in the case-studies), in different historical time (the industrial revolution, the present five-year plans), as a form of production, and as a strategy for development. Each time they meet it, the students' understanding of industrialisation should widen and deepen, until at the end they can handle it at an abstract level. Instead of just describing it, they should be able to write an essay on "How industry can help a country increase its wealth", or "How the process of industrialisation will change people's ways of living."

The diagram on the next page shows how this might work. It shows how the concepts "industry" and "industrialisation" are studied again and again throughout the syllabus, at a deeper and more abstract level each time. A teacher can also plan to "spiral" certain ideas within the different sections of the syllabus.

CONCLUSION

This approach to teaching and learning is both easier and more difficult than the "banking" approach. It involves the teacher in much careful forethought and planning. But it means that students do not have to stick rigidly to the printed syllabus or textbook, fearful to omit a detail. Providing the main concepts are understood, and the students have learnt through study of some facts and real examples to draw relevant generalisations and explain relationships, they will not only be able to pass the exam, but will also be able to participate in the process of "developing" their country.

Figure 3: A Spiral Curriculum

This idea can be applied to any other concept in the syllabus. Some of the most important ones are: **Development, Imperialism, Trade, Production, Government and Social Formation**.

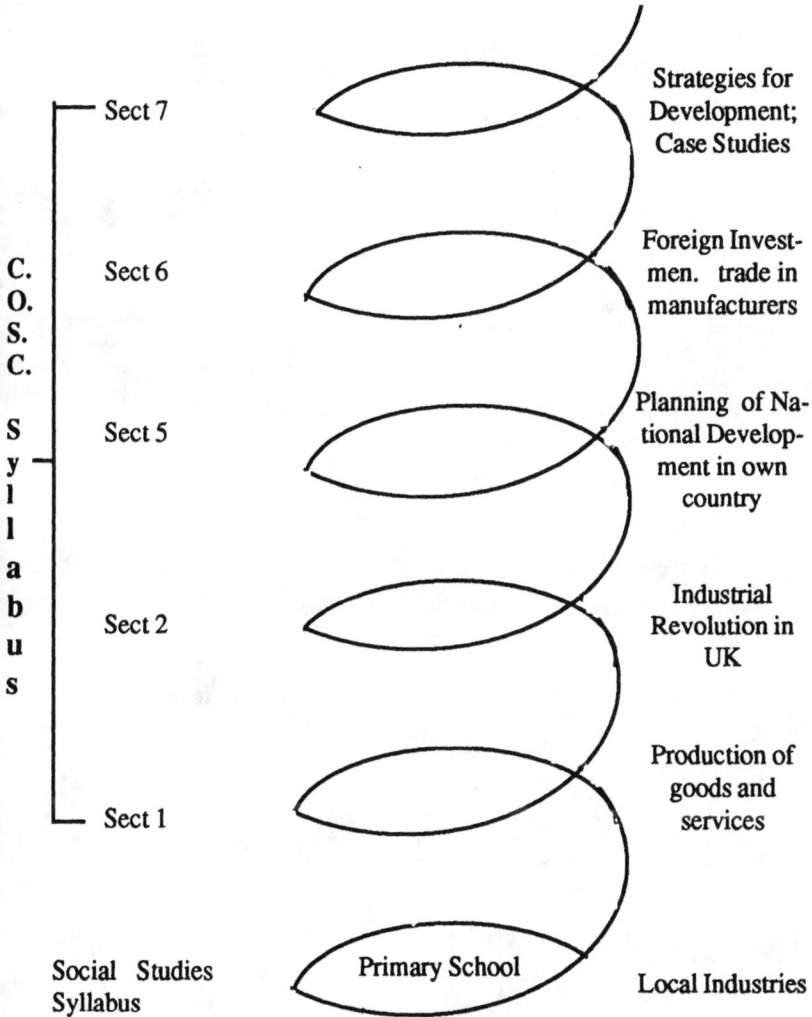

C.
O.
S.
C.

S
y
l
l
a
b
u
s

Sect 7 — Strategies for Development; Case Studies

Sect 6 — Foreign Investment. trade in manufacturers

Sect 5 — Planning of National Development in own country

Sect 2 — Industrial Revolution in UK

Sect 1 — Production of goods and services

Social Studies Syllabus — Primary School — Local Industries

13

SECTION II

PRACTICAL PROJECTS FOR
DEVELOPMENT STUDIES

"Philosophers have only interpreted the world in various ways; the point, however, is to change it". Karl Marx

One of the main objectives of the C.O.S.C. Development Studies course is to encourage students to analyse the process of "development", and to participate actively in their community's efforts to speed up that process. The students' textbook, you will find, is geared to the classroom component of the course, and this teachers' guide is mainly aimed at suggesting ways of making abstract concepts relevant to students' own experiences. But the practical side of the course - the actual involvement of students in practical experiences, in real efforts to deal with the problems confronting their communities - will require imagination, initiative and organisation on the part of the teacher.

Because the projects are supposed to be linked to the community's real needs, neither the Cambridge Exam Syndicate nor the ministry of education in any country can give specific directions about the practicals. Instead, teachers and students are encouraged to design their own projects, after evaluating the needs in their community and the resources available to them. However, it is expected that projects will fall into three broad categories.

a) Productive projects.

In these projects, students would actually be involved in some sort of production: a garden, poultry-raising, brick-making, or any other type of production for which the school has resources. The teacher could use such a project to illustrate concepts such as resources, distribution, and the use of any surplus produced; at the same time, the project would be a contribution to the productive capacity of the community, if students sold the product and perhaps donated the proceeds.

15

b) **Research projects**

Students would be expected to use their skills in gathering information, either looking at a specific community issue (for example, they might look at the existing water supply, and make recommendations for improving it) or at community resources (for example, they might look at the community's energy sources, and suggest alternatives).

c) **Community service**

Students would be expected to provide some service to their community, either as a short-term project (building a classroom, protecting springs, improving a road) or through a more long-term project (helping at the clinic; running adult literacy classes). These categories are all extremely broad, and allow a great deal of imagination on the part of teacher and students. If you are not sure whether a project will satisfy examiners, you should check proposals with the ministry of education or the Development Studies Panel in your country.

The rest of this section will suggest some of the steps you might take to get projects underway. You will note that student participation is suggested at every point in designing and implementing the practicals. Too often, practical projects are designed and imposed by the teacher - which, as many schools have discovered, can alienate students from the project, and turn the entire affair into drudgery and tedium. But workcamp projects throughout Southern Africa have shown that O-level students are perfectly capable of participating enthusiastically in development projects, provided they are volunteers. The best way to ensure this kind of enthusiasm for required practical projects, we believe, would be to allow students to participate in (ideally, to control) the whole process of designing and implementing the project. Rather than instructing students to "work" on a project they dislike, encourage students to create their own project, so that they see it as their own idea, their own contribution to development. That sense of involvement and control is more likely than anything else to encourage cheerful participation.

Of course, if your school has an on-going project, students will not be able to design all aspects of their practicals; however, you might try to encourage students to examine the project critically, discussing how it relates to the community's needs and how it might be modified to make it more useful. You may find that the process of identifying community needs, and discussing how the on-going project tries to respond to those needs, is a useful learning exercise, and can encourage students to participate actively in the project even if they did not initiate it.

Before you begin the practical project, you may want to have a tentative timetable in mind for the various stages. For example, you might plan to use four or five lessons for discussing and analysing issues in your community; four or five lessons for drawing up and discussing possible projects, and four or five lessons for evaluating the resources available for the project. Then, you could spend the rest of the year implementing the project, with a month or so at the end to evaluate it. Do not rush through the early planning stages, or through the final evaluating stage: these steps are crucial to making the practical a valuable learning experience for students.

1. NEEDS EVALUATION

You might want to begin with a discussion or series of discussions about problems facing your community. Drawing on students' knowledge of their area, you might ask the class, together or in small groups, to draw up lists of issues in their community.

These issues might range from the very abstract (for example, poverty or lack of skills) to the concrete (for example, water supply problems). Try to encourage students to be imaginative: remember, they need not discuss only solvable problems at this stage. Simply suggesting problems and discussing how different issues are linked together can be a learning exercise. Students may disagree about which problems exist; use this opportunity to promote debate in the classroom. Try to encourage students to think analytically about the problems they raise: what "causes" can they suggest? What are the effects of the problem? How are the problems linked together? How are they linked to historical processes in your area? Are these problems common, or are they specific to your community?

Try to avoid imposing your own set of priorities and ideas on the class at this point: even if you disagree about the nature of development issues facing the community, use the debate to bring in new ideas, and to encourage students to think critically about their own assumptions.

Having drawn up lists of problems, have students (as a class or in small groups) discuss each item on the list, describing its proportions, its causes and its effects on the community. You might ask each group to write reports on this process of "needs evaluation", as a way of emphasising the importance of evaluating problems critically and analytically. The entire class might then discuss the reports.

2. PROJECT PROPOSALS

Having drawn up a list of problems and carefully described them, encourage students to discuss ways of dealing with them. Have each group of students suggest several projects that could help the community overcome each of the challenges they have identified.

Obviously, the proposed projects will vary from the enormous (for example, a hydro-electric dam) to the minute (perhaps a jumble sale to raise funds for charity). Yet this, too, can become a valuable learning exercise. Encourage students to suggest a range of projects, all aimed at attacking a single problem. In addition to giving students a sense of broader issues, a range of project proposals can show that even as individuals there are many ways they can participate in "development" - and that there is no single "correct" approach to any problem

For example, students might have identified "education" as a problem in their community. In further discussion, this might be re-defined as a lack of technical skills needed for greater productivity. Projects that might attack this problem could include: a new school, new teacher training programmes, an adult literacy campaign, a new library to make reference books available; an effort to identify local skills which could be used in new, more productive ways; or an effort to inform the community about the educational programmes and resources that already exist in their community. Each of these proposals could in some way help deal with the original problem, yet they all require very different resources and activities. (You may wish to point out to students that research projects, too, can identify resources and give a better idea of the size of problems; students rarely see research as making a practical contribution to development.)

Having listed a range of possible projects, have groups of students discuss and note down the kinds of resources and activities each of their project

18

proposals would need. Try to keep proposals as realistic as possible: if they suggest building a new school, for example, have them try to find out how much it would cost to build a new school; how many teachers would be required and where they might come from; how many salaries would be paid, and how; how many students could be accommodated, and how much it would cost to provide books. In this example, they might talk to the headmaster, or write to the ministry of education for more detailed information. The more realistic the proposals are, the more students will have learned about the real world outside the classroom - which, after all, is one of the goals of practical projects.

You might also suggest that students consider alternative ways of approaching different aspects of each project proposal. For example, if hiring qualified teachers is expensive, what alternatives exist? Would these alternatives satisfy the project's original objectives? If a central library is expensive, what about setting up a mobile library to bring resources to remote areas? Here, again, you might encourage students to use their imaginatiion; ask groups to discuss each aspect of their proposal critically, to see if they cannot improve it by offering alternative forms of organisation.

3. RESOURCE EVALUATION

Having outlined project proposals, students can now begin to discuss the proposals that are within their own abilities. (Probably before you begin this step, you should decide whether you want the whole class to take on one project, or whether students will continue to work in smaller groups. You might want to ask students what they prefer, pointing out that smaller groups, almost inevitably, will mean smaller projects, but that in smaller groups everyone can participate more easily.)

Some of the projects students have outlined will quickly be identified as far beyond students' capacity - they will be too large, too expensive, too long-term. But other projects may be borderline - especially if students can propose different ways of achieving the same ends. Try not to dismiss any proposals too quickly: see if students cannot suggest ways of implementing each project that would put the proposal within the class's means.

Of course, you will also have to discuss the resources available to the class, and possible ways of increasing those resources. Some of the constraints facing you, and some possible ways of overcoming them, are listed below.

a)   **Time:** Time-tabling of practicals is often a real problem in formal school systems, especially if the project is not one that can be done for an hour a week but needs fairly consistent work. A garden, for example, will need regular watering and weeding. An adult literacy programme will need time for classes - at hours that working adults can attend. Some ways around the time-tabling problem might be: a rota system, where each student gives up some free time each month; doing the project on weekends, free afternoons, or evenings; or planning a project for the school holidays, so that it can be a concerted effort for a week or two rather than dragging on throughout the school year. (Remember that projects may have different time requirements at different points: you may need a full week to get started, and then one afternoon every week to continue.)

b)   **Skills:** Many project proposals will call for skills and knowledge that neither the students nor teachers possess, but many of these skills will be available in your community: other teachers, students' parents, and members of the community may have the skills you lack, and may be willing to advise a group of students. Other advice may also be gained from reference books. For example, the EDA *People's Workbook* (available from EDA, Box 62054, Marshalltown 2107, Johannesburg) gives a great deal of easily-digestible information on many practical projects for Southern Africa. Other information might also be obtained from agricultural and health extension workers, ministry publications and school libraries. Encourage students to seek out and use the skills available in the community, rather than accepting limitations.

c)   **Resources:** If students decide to embark on projects that require money, tools and other resources beyond the amount budgeted, you may want to consider ways of raising funds. Some methods of fund-raising include the following:

i)   Seeking donations. Many groups such as Chambers of Commerce or individual businesses are willing to sponsor school activities. Aid agencies and foreign embassies often have funds for small local projects. Have students draw up a project proposal and take it round to potential donors. Individuals may also be willing to donate funds or equipment.

20

ii)   Raising funds through student activities.

There are many ways for students to raise money, by offering any of several services to the community. Discuss possible methods with students, and see if they are willing to undertake such activities. See if they can suggest other activities. (If students live in a very poor area, such an attempt may be difficult; discuss these constraints with students before undertaking such efforts.)

There may be other ways for your class to find the funds and equipment needed for your project; encourage students to approach these problems imaginatively.

4. IMPLEMENTATION

Having identified your objectives, methods of tackling the problem, and resources available, the class or groups of students should design the project's implementation. Some of the steps in this stage should include those listed below.

a) A tentative schedule for carrying out the project, noting different phases, and leaving time for a final evaluation.

b) Collecting resources. Make sure students organise carefully who will be responsible for collecting resources, and how they will be collected. Make sure everyone understands and is willing to undertake their assigned aspect of project. (Again, some sort of schedule for this stage of the project may keep it from dragging on for months).

c) Implementation. Students should have a clear idea of the project goals and of how they plan to reach them. As much as possible, students should be responsible for organising and carrying out the entire activity.

5. EVALUATION

Throughout the process of designing and carrying out the project, students will have to identify problems and possible solutions. Not only at the initial stages of setting up the project, but throughout implementation, students will have to resolve problems blocking the project's success. In fact, many student projects may not achieve their goals. **This need not mean, however, that the project is a failure.** Keep reminding students that the practical component of Development Studies is meant as a learning exercise; if problems ultimately block the project's completion, that need not make the whole exercise useless. As the process of analysing and solving problems is emphasised, students should view their project "journal" as an on-going and essential aspect of the project. At its best, the journal can serve as an important link between the classroom and practical components of the course. Students should be encouraged to note down every event in the course of the project, and try to discuss how these events are linked to wider processes in the community, or to abstract concepts discussed in the classroom.

(This process can also assist in classroom discussions, if students are encouraged to offer examples from their practical experience to illustrate abstract concepts. For example, a common problem in many practicals may be that girls and boys are assigned different types of chores; students may be willing to examine their own attitudes critically in class. Try not to cut such discussions short; they may prove to be the most immediate learning experience in Development Studies.)

Throughout the period of implementation, check that students are keeping their journals up to date. You might insist that they make a few notes after every practical period; these notes can later be written up more fully. However, the fuller these early notes are, the more thorough the final journal will be. Encourage students in each group to share their observations with each other; such discussions can often push analysis much further than individual students are likely to get.

Another way of encouraging critical analysis might be to ask groups of students to report back to the class at regular intervals. Again, this can encourage discussions, and force individuals to look at their projects in new ways.

SECTION III

CLASS ACTIVITIES

Note: **The numbers that appear next to each section heading refer to the relevant pages in the textbook** *Working for the Future*

Chapter 1: Production

Needs and Wants (7-8)

Have each student list needs and wants, and the goods and services needed to satisfy these needs and wants. Then have students compare these lists, first in small groups, then as a class. Try to establish which are basic needs - necessary for physical survival - and which are "wants" that might vary from person to person.

Discuss the following questions with the students:

1.   What are the differences between "needs" and "wants"? Why are these distinctions often made?

2.   What are the differences between goods and services?

3.   How are needs and wants affected by people's environments? How do people learn from each other about goods they might "need", or about the ways in which needs can be fulfilled? For example, if students had lived 100 years ago, would they have listed "cars" as one of their needs? How do needs and wants change?

4.   How are needs and wants affected by people's culture? Are the needs actually affected, or only the way in which the needs are fulfilled?

Factors of Production (8-11)

Bring in any object - a book or a cup will do - and discuss the raw materials and labour needed to produce the object. Some important points to include in the discussion are listed below.

1.   The labour needed: both the time and skills needed to make the object, or to make machines that helped make the object.

2.   The raw materials used: where they might have been found; the labour and machines needed to get them and process them, and how they were brought to a factory producing the final object (transport).

3.   The machines used in the process, and the factors of production that went into producing these machines. Make sure students understand the concept of capital, and how money can be used to gain access to capital goods. Make sure students understand why some economists view capital as labour and raw materials that have been transformed into money or goods. Make sure students understand the difference between theories that view entrepreneurship as a fourth factor of production, and those that consider it part of all people's make-up.

Background: see discussion in Ann Seidman, Chapter 3. (Details of this book and others mentioned in the guide can be found in Section IV below: "Background Material for Teachers")

Resources in the Classroom

Have students (singly or in small groups) make and compare lists of the raw materials used in making their classroom. Discuss:

a)   where the raw materials came from;

b)   the processes these raw materials must have gone through to be made into usable goods, and

c)   other ways in which the same goods might have been made, either from the same raw materials or using other, locally available resources.

Local Raw Materials

Have students make and compare lists of raw materials that are found locally. Some of the following might be mentioned: land; water; solar energy; local mineral deposits; wood and animal manure. Discuss:

a)   how these resources are used to produce goods and services for people;

b)   other ways the same resources might be used, to produce other goods, and

c)   local resources that might exist, but which are not being fully exploited - for example, land that is unused because it lacks irrigation; mines that have not been worked to full capacity. Discuss the inputs would be needed for full utilisation of raw materials.

Technological Processes (A)

Have students compare different technological processes for making goods which are similar. Ask students to suggest examples, such as hand-made clay pots and manufactured metal ones, handspun cloth and machine-made cloth, simple wood fires and electric stoves. Discuss:

a)   the levels of labour and skills required for different types of technology;

a)   the raw materials needed for different processes;

b)   the kinds of energy (human, electricity, gas) needed for different technologies, and

c)   the types of machinery needed for different processes.

You may want to bring in some of the following concepts: labour vs capital intensive technology; 'intermediate' vs. complex technology, and appropriate use of local skills and resources.

MAKING AND IMPROVING - Simulation Game

Purpose: to provide an opportunity for students to experience non-verbally some basic economic concepts, such as "raw material"," "investment", "capital", "currency", "division of labour". The activity also provides practice in quick decision-making, in discussion skills, and in seeing problems as a whole rather than in fragments.

Material needed: pencils; sheets of ordinary white paper; sheets of sticky coloured paper; scissors; stock of home-made paper money; sets of templates, made out of stiff card, giving outlines of car, television set, television screen, and star. There must be one set for each group taking part in the activity. The template for the car should be roughly twice the area of the TV-set template.

Procedure:

1.   Divide into two or more teams; at least two students must also act as the "market-place".

2.   Give each team 20 units of currency. Students representing the "market-place" get the scissors, paper, pencils and templates.

3.   Explain the rules:

a)   five minutes are given during which each team can discuss what it will do.

b)   fifteen minutes are given during which the teams can make and trade. All buying is from the market-place, and all selling is to the market-place, at the following rates: (put the list on the blackboard)

templates: 4 units each
scissors and pencils: 3 units each
sheets of ordinary white paper: 1 unit
sticky coloured paper: 1 unit
television cut out of white paper: 1 unit
white television with coloured screen: 2 units
car out of white paper: 3 units
white car with coloured star on its bonnet: 4 units

c)   after 15 minutes of trade and making, add up points of each team according to "wealth", including currency and "stock", using process above.

(Note: students may not use pencils, papers or scissors other than those bought from the market-place).

Discussion

Some of the questions that could be explored during discussion after the game are listed below.

1.   What aspects of the real world were dramatised - such as raw material, capital, investment, mass production, manufactured goods? What do the various items used (templates, scissors, currency) represent?

2.   What methods were employed by the winning team? Did they win through good luck, or through good management? How did they make the decisions they did? Did they behave in ways that other teams would describe as selfish or unfair?

3.   How did students feel about the jobs they found themselves doing? What were the most interesting and enjoyable jobs? Did everyone have something to do, or were there pockets of unemployment? Were human resources all being used efficiently?

A fundamental human activity is to process raw materials in some way, and to consume them. But who decides what raw materials should be used? Who decides how they should be processed? How they should be consumed? What are the different ways in which different societies have arranged these matters? What are the main ways in which humans have found raw materials and bought, borrowed, begged or stolen raw materials?

Acknowledgement: *Learning for Change in World Society* by Robin Richardson. Published by World Studies Project, London 1974.

27

Technological Processes (B)

Ask students to observe and take notes on a local production process, such as a farm or factory nearby. Ask them to write descriptions of what they see, noting the raw materials used, the machines and tools used, the labour and skills needed, the division of labour in the process, and other ways in which the same type of goods could be made, using different raw materials or different technologies.

Discuss the descriptions in class. Note other ways in which production might have been organised; for example, would the technology and the division of labour have been different if the enterprise had been co-operatively owned? How might it have been organized to reduce boredom? How might it have been made more efficient? How else might the same raw materials have been used? Who decided how and what should be made? Was that the best way for such important decisions to be made?

Division of Labour (A) (12-13)

Ask students to list the chores each member of their family does at home.

Discuss the questions below.

1.   How do they think the chores were divided up? (The family decided cooperatively, a parent decided, etc.)

2.   Are special skills required for each task? Could the father do the cooking? Why or why not?

3.   Is this division of labour efficient? Would a more or less flexible division of chores be more efficient?

4.   How do stereotypes of male and female work affect the division of labour within the family?

Division of Labour (B)

Ask students to observe and describe division of labour in local productive enterprises. Discuss these descriptions, noting how tasks are divided up, who makes these decisions, whether the division is efficient, and how it might be made more productive.

Discuss the problem of boredom with an extreme division of labour (see your textbook: box on page 13). Ask students whether it is more important for workers to enjoy their work, or to produce more. Why?

Consumption and Investment (A) (11-12)

Discuss the box on page 12, about the farmer's decision about how to use the extra harvest. Ask students what the farmer should do, and why.

Ask students if they have ever had to choose (or if their parents have had to choose) between consuming and investing a surplus. What have they usually done? Why?

Consumption and Investment (B) (13-17)

Look with students at the charts of the cycles of poverty (p13) and of hunger (p17). Ask students what the similarities and differences between the charts are. Note that lower nutrition levels mean lower energy, and less production; in the same way, lower incomes mean people can invest less, and produce less. Ask students:

a)   whether they have known any cases of malnutrition, and what was done about them, and

b)   whether they know of any cases where more investment could have increased production (and future consumption).

Discuss with students how the choice between investment and consumption relates to:

a)   levels to which basic needs are fulfilled (whether there is some surplus left over for investment);

b)   levels to which wants are fulfilled;

c)   the amount of surplus available for investment and

d)   the existence of opportunities for investment.

29

CONSUMPTION AND INVESTMENT - Simulation Game

Purpose

To illustrate the impact of family size on the surplus available for investment, showing how larger families must spend more on basic needs, and have little left for investment in production.

Materials needed

100 markers (squares of paper, or paper-clips) for each group in the class.

Procedure:

1.   Divide the class into small groups, ranging in size from three to eight students (make sure the groups are not equal in size).

2.   Give each group 100 markers. This represents their "family" income of $100.

3.   Discuss with students what the annual expenses for the "family" should be, and how many markers each member requires. For example, your list might include:

food	$5 per family member
shelter	$2 per family member
clothes	$3 per family member
school fees	$2 per family member
recreation	$1 per family member
medicine	$1 per family member

4.   For each "family" member, have the group set aside enough markers to cover their expenses.

5.   Compare the different "surpluses" left after basic expenses

have been covered. (For the list above, a "family" of three will have spent $43, and should have 57 markers left, while a "family" of eight will have spent $112, and will be 12 markers in debt.)

Discussion

What does this game tell students about the problem of family size and available surplus for investment? What does it tell them about the choices open to people?

Ownership and Employment (A) (15-18)

Discuss with students the history of labour migration in Southern Africa (see the box on page 17), and in your region in particular. Ask students why they think people went to work on the mines. Why they didn't stay home and farm? Would the students like to work as migrant labourers? Why or why not? What does this situation tell us about the differences between people who have taken control of natural resources and those who have not?

Background reading: L. Callinicos.

Ownership and Employment (B)

DEBATE TOPIC: "PEOPLE ARE POOR BECAUSE THEY DON'T WORK HARD"

Some points you might bring up in the discussion include those below.

1.   People who are poor have nothing to invest.

2.   People who have no property may have a hard time borrowing money to buy raw materials or capital equipment (see chart on p.13.)

3.   People who already have money or property can use it to make more.

4.   People who are poor must rely on what they can earn in wages, because without capital or resources, they cannot produce very much for themselves.

Try to get students thinking about why some people have more money and property than others, and how this may give them more power in the community and over others.

Ownership and Employment (C)

Ask students to find out who owns nearby enterprises (assign them to shops, workshops, and factories in the area). Have them try to find out who owns the equipment and the tools used. Who buys the raw materials? Who owns the building? Who does the actual labour (making or selling goods)? How are wages for the labourers set?

Have students report back to class, and discuss the following questions.

1.   What they have learned about ownership patterns: did most people in their community own their own enterprises, or do they work for other people? How did these patterns come about?

2.   How did some people get enough "capital" to start projects?

3.   If there were any co-operatives in the survey, discuss the differences between cooperatives and private enterprises. Who owns tools and decides what and how much should be produced? Who benefits from increased production? Do co-operative members view their work differently from workers in ordinary wage employment?

COOPERATION: "GETTING IT TOGETHER" - Simulation Game

Purpose: To provide an opportunity for students to experience non-verbally some of the problems involved in co-operation, empathy, participation, being a member of a group, sharing, and seeing a problem as a whole.

Materials needed: For each group of five students in the class, follow these steps:

1. Rule five squares on card or stiff paper, each of identical size; about 12 centimeters square is convenient.

2. Rule each square into a pattern, as shown in the diagram: (the ratio from this diagram to the 12 cm squares will be 4:1. Measurements must be made carefully)

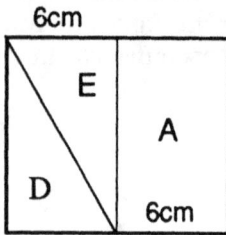

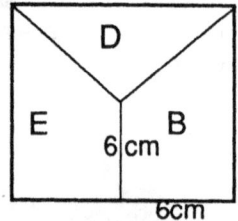

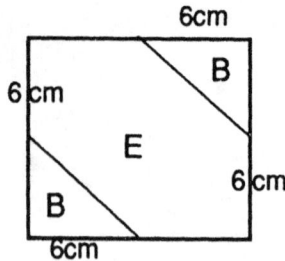

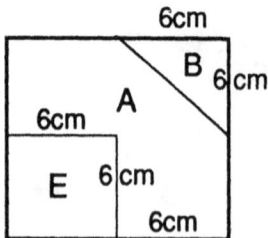

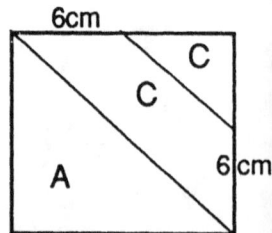

3.   Mark the smaller shapes with a letter, as shown in the diagram.

4.   Cut the squares into shapes.

5.   Group the shapes into five sets, according to their letters.

6.   Put these five sets into five envelopes, marking the envelopes with the appropriate letters.

Procedure

1.   Divide students into groups of five, and give each group a full set of envelopes marked A, B, C, D, E.

2.   Explain these rules carefully, making sure students understand. (You may want to write them on the blackboard):

a)   when the exercise starts, but not before, students should take out the contents of their envelopes.

b)   the exercise will continue until each member of the group has a complete square; the five squares in each group must all be the same size.

c)   students may pass cards to other members of their group, but they may not reach out and take one.

d)   there must be no talking during the exercise, nor any other kind of communication - no winks, gestures, shakes or nods of heads, etc.

e)   students may at any time decline to take further part in the exercise.
The teacher also has the right to stop the exercise at any time.

3.   What actually happens: Inevitably, in every group, a square is formed that is the right size, but which is not one of the ones shown in the diagram above. This means that although one student has a

complete square in front of him or her, others in the group will be unable to complete their squares - and since they cannot discuss the problem, the whole exercise will be held up until the person with the wrong square recognises he or she has taken a piece that someone else needs, and gives it up.

Discussion

A good way to start discussion is to ask groups to discuss what actually happened during the exercise, and how they felt about it. What were the hold-ups? Breakthroughs? Did people feel frustrated and irritated when they couldn't find the pieces they needed, or communicate with others in the group? Did the people who couldn't complete a square feel anxious? Envious? Did the people who finished early feel self-satisfied and complacent? Did people find it difficult to think of their project as a co-operative one, rather than an individual one? Did the person who had to dismantle a wrong square feel as if he or she was sacrificing something for the group? How did they feel at the end?

Ask students to discuss what they learned through the exercise about sharing, or aid (the difference between real insightful generosity and just discarding something), and about democratic participation and co-operation. Are there tensions between individual self-satisfaction and co-operation?

Acknowledgement: In its basic format, this exercise was first published in the NEA Journal, USA, October 1969.

Infrastructure (19)

Have students draw maps showing your country's physical infrastructure: major roads, railway lines, ports and airports. You will be able to refer back to these maps when discussing the chapter on Government.

Discuss with students what the maps show about the development and exploitation of resources. How do roads and railway lines help develop an area? Who decided where the roads and railways should be built? Are there other ways to make such decisions?

If possible, ask someone from your local ministry of public works to come to class to talk about how your government decides where to put new roads, etc. On what basis are such decisions made?

Distribution Networks (19-20)

Give each student or group of students a short list of goods that are widely available. Send each group to different shops to find the prices of these items. Compare the results: is one shop generally more expensive than others? Why might this be so? Who sets prices, and how are such decisions made?

Discuss where the goods come from. How do shopkeepers know what to sell? Where do they get them? How are they brought to the shop? Some of the concepts you may wish to bring into the discussion here include, wholesale, retail, transportation and communication systems, imports and exports.

Development Strategies (A) (23-28)

Make sure students understand the basic differences between capitalist and socialist approaches to development strategies.

Under Capitalism

- Resources are privately owned.

- Individual "entrepreneurs" or "capitalists" make production decisions.

- Profits are considered a necessary reward to motivate entrepreneurs.

- Governments usually try to stay out of production, although their decisions about infrastructure, subsidies, etc., have major importance for economic development (see chapter on Government).

- The goal for development strategies is economic growth and expanded productive capacities; benefits are expected to "trickle down" to the rest of society.

Under Socialism

- Major resources are "nationalised": they are controlled by the state, which is supposed to represent the people.

- The government makes most major production decisions: what and how much to produce.

- People tend to work co-operatively; there are no owners and workers.

- "Profits" for private capitalists are considered exploitative, not just a return for investment and reward for entreprenueurship.

- The goal for development strategies is to increase productive capacity, **and** to insure improvements in everyone's quality of life.

Of course there are many other important differences, such as the different emphasis on education and social services, etc. You may wish to bring these kinds of differences up now, or wait until later in the course when you're dealing more specifically with such issues.

Background: see Ann Seidman, Chapter 2.

Development Strategies (B)

Discuss your country's development strategies; if available, get your country's development plan (usually available at the government printers) and discuss the broad outlines of it with your students. Remember that you will discuss it again and again during the course; this is only the introduction, so don't overwhelm students with too many details. However, ask students to think about which aspects of your government's strategy are capitalist, which are socialist, and how well they fit together. In particular, look at the strategy's goals, at patterns of ownership, and at the kind of enterprises the government is trying to support.

Development Strategies (C)

DEBATE: "PLANNED ECONOMIES TEND TO IGNORE INDIVIDUALS' NEEDS; A CAPITALIST APPROACH, BASED ON INDIVIDUAL ENTREPRENEURS, IS MORE LIKELY TO RESPOND TO PEOPLE'S WISHES".

Here are some points you might try to bring out in the discussion and debate.

Pro

-       Individual entrepreneurs can respond quickly to market pressures and to consumers' demands.

-       Governments are hard to control, and often don't respond to people's needs.

-       Unless you reward individual entrepreneurs with "profits", they won't try to produce efficiently.

Con

-       Individuals won't use the resources of the country for everyone's benefit; it's better to have the government make production decisions.

-       Unless the government plans what and how much should be produced, goods will be produced that an elite can afford, but which are beyond the reach of most people.

-      Governments may be hard to control, but at least they are ultimately responsible for the general welfare, while individual capitalists are only working for themselves.

-      People work better co-operatively than as individuals, and profits to individuals are not necessarily the best incentive.

FIELD TRIPS

Take students to one, or several, productive enterprises in the community. Before going, draw up a list together of questions they should ask during the trip. Afterwards, discuss their answers together, and compile a class report on the trip. These are some of the questions students should be asking.

1.   What is being produced?
2.   What raw materials are used?
3.   What capital (machinery) is used?
4.   Where do the raw materials come from?
5.   Where did the initial capital for the enterprise come from?
6.   What skills are needed to produce the goods?
7.   Who provides the labour - the owner, or hired workers?
8.   Who owns the project?
9.   Why was the particular good chosen to be produced?
10.   Who buys it?
11.   Where is it sold?
12.   How much training do workers get? How much are they paid?
13.   What other goods could be made from the same raw materials and labour?
14.   What other ways might the production process be organised? What different technologies might be used? What about a co-operative enterprise? etc.

Note: At the end of the classroom activities for Chapter 3 (see below) a very similar Field Trip is suggested. Teachers may wish to omit one of the trips or combine the two

Chapter 2: Changing Societies

Hunter-Gatherer Soceiities (A) (31-34)

Discuss with students some aspects of the lives of hunter-gatherers. Often they will have prejudices and stereotypes against the San, particularly. Try to explore the bases of these, and deal with them.

You might want to focus the discussion particularly upon the following issues.

1.   Interaction with the environment; bring in the concept of conservation as a kind of investment in the future productivity of an area.

2.   Decision-making in small egalitarian groups.

3.   Level of productivity: why did hunter-gatherers keep such a low level of productivity and technology for centuries? Why might they prefer to live as they do?

4.   Religion and ritual: look at the role of religion in keeping the group together, and at the way hunter-gatherers have to co-operate to survive.

Background: Stephens, Minority Rights Group *Report on the San.*

Hunters-Gatherer Societies (B)

DEBATE: "THE SAN WHO STILL LEAD TRADITIONAL LIVES SHOULD BE LEFT ALONE, AND NOT FORCED TO JOIN MODERN SOCIETY"

Here are some points that might be brought up.

Pro

-     San do not have the skills needed to succeed in the industrialised world; they will automatically be disadvantaged and exploited.

41

-       San are fine as they are, and they don't bother anyone; why should we impose our values?

-       The San culture shouldn't be allowed to die.

-       Many San don't want to change.

Con

-       The industrialised world is here, whether we want it or not; it will eventually envelop the San's territory anyway.

-       Leaving the San alone will not help them; since integration is probably inevitable anyway, it is better to teach them now and to help them integrate into the new world than it would be to leave them to be integrated when they're at a disadvantage.

-       Preserving the culture can be done through museums, films, and by encouraging San children to learn as much as they can of their old lifestyles at the same time as they learn "modern" skills; otherwise we're just building a human zoo.

Transition to Agriculture (34-36)

Discuss the relation between changes in technology, levels of surplus available to a community, and differences within the community. Give local examples if possible, such as the rise of an aristocratic class.

Discuss the differences between hunter-gatherer societies and agricultural communities, and how people's lives change with the discoveries of farming and iron-working (see the box on page 47).

Shifting Cultivation

Discuss with students:

a)   reasons for shifting cultivation in Southern Africa (soil, climate);

b)   the impact of shifting cultivation on local culture (types of shelter,

:and ownership patterns, power of chiefs), and

c)   the role of cattle in local society - why do cattle become such an important sign of wealth when people move fields often? (Is it because it is the only wealth they can carry with them? Because it is less plentiful than land?)

Ask students to imagine and discuss their ancestors' confusion when the first Europeans arrived, with their notions of private land-ownership.

Local History (A)

Discuss with students:

a)   the arrival of Bantu-speaking people in their area;
b)   the arrival of iron-working skills in their area; and
d)   the impact on local culture of agriculture and iron-working. Are there any beliefs or rituals connected with either (such as Incwala)?

Background: see N. Parsons, Chapter 1

Local History (B)

As a class, discuss and draw a time-line on newsprint, showing dates of major significance for your region. Some dates you might want to include could be (have students do research to find dates):

a)   earliest human inhabitants of the region;
b)   earliest signs of domesticated animals;
c)   earliest signs of agricultural techniques;
d)   early signs of iron-working;
e)   arrival of Bantu-speaking peoples in area;
f)   beginnings of long-distance trade;
g)   rise of any large states based on trade;
h)   impact of Mfecane/Difaqane in your area;
i)   early European contacts;
j)   any resistance to colonial rule;
k)   beginning of colonial administration;
l)   rise of nationalist movement;
m)   any important dates in independence struggle, and

n)   independence and important events since independence.

For example,   part of a time-line for the Bulawayo region is shown opposite.

Local Culture

Divide students into groups of three or four. Have each group research and report on some aspect of local tradition, such as marriage rituals, dances, communal labour or musical forms. If possible, ask students to enact rituals for the class.

Religion (32, box)

DEBATE: "RELIGIONS ARE OFTEN WAYS TO KEEP A COMMUNITY TOGETHER, BY ENFORCING CUSTOMS".

Witchcraft (41, box)

Ask students if they know of any incidents of spells or witchcraft. For each incident they report, discuss:

a)   whether the fear of magic did not play a part in the spells' success;

b)   whether the witchcraft was used to punish someone for behaving badly in terms of the group's customs;

c)   whether the magic was used to gain power over someone or something that is normally outside human control, and

d)   whether the magic could not be explained in scientific terms.

Long Distance Trade and Empires (44-45)

Look at maps of ancient trade routes in Africa (pp 48-49). Discuss with

44

Figure 4: Time line for Bulawayo region

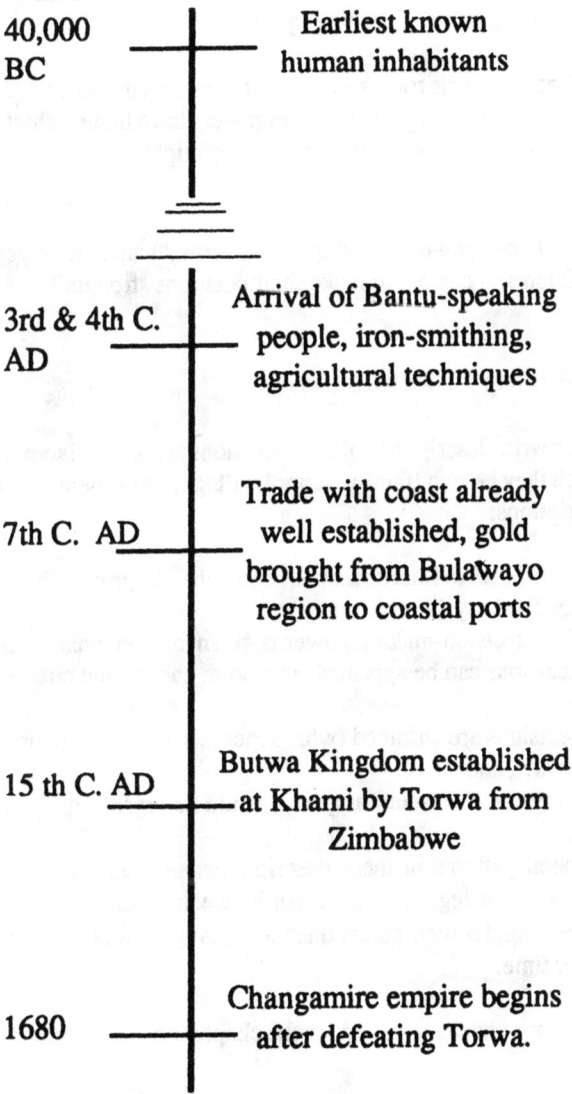

40,000 BC	Earliest known human inhabitants
3rd & 4th C. AD	Arrival of Bantu-speaking people, iron-smithing, agricultural techniques
7th C. AD	Trade with coast already well established, gold brought from Bulawayo region to coastal ports
15 th C. AD	Butwa Kingdom established at Khami by Torwa from Zimbabwe
1680	Changamire empire begins after defeating Torwa.

Background: N. Parsons, passim

students the issues below.

1.   The rise of long-distance trade: what were traders seeking from Africa? What did they bring in return? What does the fact that luxuries were purchased tell us about the African Kingdoms?

2.   Links between trade routes and sites of African Kingdoms: how did kings take control? How might taxes from traders have helped chiefs pay armies and become more powerful? How or why might such empires have fallen?

3)   Links between power and religion: how might ancient kings have used law, religion and custom to make their positions stronger?

Decision-Making Processes (43-44)

Ask students to write descriptions of how decisions are made in some small group to which they belong (family, school, village). Ask them to discuss in these descriptions:

a)   who contributes to final decisions about what the groups should do;
b)   who has final say (if anyone);
c)   how final decision-making power is given, and on what basis;
d)   how decisions can be appealed (to whom, under what circumstances);
e)   how decisions are enforced (what sanctions are used against offenders?), and
f)   other ways in which similar groups could be organised.

Look for general patterns in these descriptions, such as links between economic power and legal power, links between traditional decision-making processes and contemporary ones, and changes in decision-making processes over time.

These descriptions should be saved for the chapter on Government.

STAR POWER - Simulation Game

This is a game in which a low mobility three-tiered society is built through the distribution of wealth in the form of chips. Participants have a chance to progress from one level of society to another by acquiring wealth through trading with other participants. Once the society is established, the group with the most wealth is given the right to make the rules for the game. They generally make rules which the other groups consider to be unfair, fascistic and racist. A revolt against the rules and the rule-makers generally ensues. When this occurs the game is ended. The game is useful for raising questions about the uses of power in a competitive society.

Dividing the participants and assigning chips

The participants are divided into three approximately equal groups named Squares, Circles and Triangles. Each person wears a symbol representing his group, i.e. the Squares wear a square symbol, the Circles a circular symbol and the Triangles a triangular symbol.

Each participants is given five chips. Each Square receives one gold chip, one green chip and the remaining three randomly selected from the colours red, white and blue. Each Circle is given one green chip and the remaining four selected from the colours red, white and blue. The Triangles are given random assortment of red, white and blue chips. The only exception to this distribution is that one Circle and one Triangle receive the same distribution as the squares, i.e. one gold, one green and a random assortment of red, white and blue.

Determining the chips required for a game

The **total** number of chips required equals: 5 x number of partici-pants.

The number of **gold** chips required equals: the number of Squares plus 2.

The number of **green** chips required equals: the number of Squares plus the number of Circles plus 1.

The number of **red, white** and **blue** chips required equals: 5 x number of participants minus the total number of green and gold chips required. There should be about an **equal number** of red, white and blue chips.

Example: Suppose you have 34 people and divide them into 12 Squares, 12 Circles and 10 Triangles. The total number of chips required equals: 5 x 34 or 170. The total number of **gold** chips required equals: 12 (the number of Squares) plus 2 = 14. The total number of **green** chips required equals: 12 (the number of Squares) plus 12 (the number of Circles) plus 1 = 25. The total number of **red, white** or **blue** chips required equals: 170 minus (14 + 25) = 131 which means about 44 of each colour.

Explaining the rules

1.   Tell the participants that this is a game that involves trading and bargaining and that the three persons with the highest scores will be declared the winner. They will probably ask later in the game if there is going to be a group winner. The answer is: "The three individuals with the highest scores will be declared the winner." **Do not** tell them that a group is going to be given the right to make the rules of the game.

2.   Explain the following scoring system to the participants:

every gold chip is worth 50 points;
every green chip is worth 25 points;
every red chip is worth 15 points;
every white chip is worth 10 points;
every blue chip is worth 5 points.

Additional points are given if a person is able to get several points of the same colour:

five chips of the same colour are worth 20 points;

four chips of the same colour are worth 10 points;
three chips of the same colour are worth 5 points; and
no extra points given for two chips of the same colour.

Example:

A person's total score if he had 5 gold chips would be 250 plus 20 for 5 chips of the same colour for a total of 270 points. If he had four blue chips and one red chip, his score would equal 4 x 5 (for the blue chips) plus 15 (for the red chip) plus 10 points for distribution of the same colour for a total of 45 points. Three reds and two blues would equal 45 + 5 + 10 or 60 points. Five reds: 75 + 20 or 95 points.

3.   Distribute the chips as outlined previously to the Squares, Circles and Triangles.

4.   Explain the following rules of bargaining.

a)   They have 7 minutes to improve their scores.

b)   They improve their scores by trading advantageously with other Squares, Circles and Triangles.

c)   All chips should be hidden. (**This rule should be strictly enforced**).

d)   There is no talking unless hands are touching. (**This rule should be strictly enforced**)

e)   Persons must be holding hands to effect a trade.

f)   Once participants touch the hand of another participant a chip of unequal value or colour must be traded. If a couple cannot consummate a trade they may have to hold hands for the entire ten minutes trading session.

g)   Persons with folded arms do not have to trade with other persons.

h)   Only one for one trades are legal. Two for one or any other combinations are illegal. Chips **must** be of different colours.

i)   Do not reveal that the Squares are given chips of a higher value than the Circles or Triangles.

j)   Add other rules that you deem appropriate.

Start the trading session

1.   After the rules have been explained, start the trading session. Tell them it will last 7 minutes.

2.   During the trading session, your assistant should be putting each participant's initials on the blackboard.

3.   After 7 minutes of trading session, have each group return to their circle of chairs.

4.   Have the participants compute their scores for the trading session, record them on their score sheet and hand the score sheet to your assistant.

5.   Have your assistant record the scores on the blackboard opposite the person's initials. (The initials and their scores can be put on by the participants themselves if an assistant is not available.)

6.   Explain the following rules for the **bonus points session**.

a)   Hold up a bonus chip (a double chip) and tell them that this is a bonus point chip.

b)   Give each group three chips.

c)   Tell them that each chip is worth 20 points.

d)   Their task during the bonus session is to distribute the bonus chips to members of their group.

e)   The chips must be distributed in units of 20 or more, that is, one person might receive all 3 bonus chips, and 60 points or 3 people might receive 1 chip each worth 20 points, but 6 people could not receive 10 points each.

f)   They have five minutes to distribute the bonus chips. If the groups have not distributed the chips at the end of the five minutes, the points will be taken back by the director and no one will receive them.

g)   The decision regarding the distribution of chips must be by unanimous vote.

h)   Participants can eliminate people from their group by a majority vote. (Eliminated people can form another group.) They should be a Triangle group.

7.   Answer any questions.

8.   Start the bonus points session.

9.   After about five minutes, end the bonus points session.

10.   Have those people who receive bonus points record them on the blackboard opposite their initials, and give back bonus chips.

11.   Put those people with the highest total scores in the square group. If there is a Circle or a Triangle who has a higher score than a Square, have them trade groups. Any changes should be announced to the group and it should be generally made known that so and so who was a Square has become a Circle, because they did not receive enough points, and so and so who was a Circle is now a Square because they received a higher number of points than a Square. In any event, **it is important that the group know that the squares are made up of those people with the highest scores.**

12.   Start the second round

Note: Repeat this cycle - bargaining session, bonus session, reclas- sification - once or twice or until the participants understand the process and the fact that the Squares are high scorers.

13.   After about the second bonus session, announce that the Squares now have the authority to make the rules for the game and that while any group can suggest rules for the game the Squares will decide which rules will be implemented. You might tell the Squares that they might want to make rules like re-distributing the chips on a more equal basis, requiring Triangles and Circles to bargain with the Squares even though they have their arms folded, or requiring Triangles and Circles to give Squares the chips they ask for regardless of whether they wish to trade or not. Announce any rules that the Squares establish to all the participants unless they want them kept a secret.

14.   From then on, play it by ear

What is likely to happen is that the Squares will make very tough rules that protect their own power. This has happened in every organised group that we have played it with so far. The Circles and Triangles will either give up, organise, become hostile, or commit an act of frustration and defiance. Stop the game when it is evident that the Squares have made rules which the others consider unfair and fascistic. This is generally after two to four rounds. After the game gather the group together and discuss the implications of the game for the real world.

Discussion

Here are some questions you might want to discuss at the end of the game.

1.   Are there any parallels between the system set up by the game and the system or sub-systems in which we live?

2.   Does the game say anything about the nature of man?

3.   Is it the nature of man to seek inequality, to attempt to be better than his fellow man, to seek for more privileges and wealth? If yes, is there anything wrong with such strivings? Can they be legitimised? Is there a moral alternative to man's search for inequality?

4.　　Would it have made much difference if the people who were the Circles had been the Squares?

5.　　Were the Squares acting with legitimate authority?

6.　　Are there any parallels between the game and the race problem, the students' problems, the problems faced by our predecessors?

7.　　If an entire group acts in unison, such as the Circles and Triangles do in going against the squares, do their actions have more legitimacy?

Acknowledgement: Game by R. Garry Shirts

Types of Shelter - Survey

Divide students into groups of two or three, and assign each group to survey housing in different parts of your community. Ask each group to find out from occupants of three houses in their area:

a)   type of material used (brick, thatch, mud, etc.);
b)   number of occupants;
c)   number of rooms;
d)   owner of house;
e)   amount of rent paid, if any;
f)   if the occupants own the house, how they acquired the land;
g)   water supply to house (communal tap, internal plumbing, etc.);
h)   cooking facilities (fire, stove, electric burner);
i)   electricity supply and
j)   method of transport usually used by family (walking, bus, car or bicycle).

Discuss the survey in class; have students see if it reveals any patterns in their community, such as:

a)   grouping of lower income and upper income housing together (why might this be true?);

b)   conditions in different areas such as materials used, crowding, number of rented and owner-built houses, and

c)   services to lower-income areas compared to upper-income such as electricity, water, roads and transport systems.

FIELD TRIPS

Take students to local historical sites, such as rock paintings, old iron smelters, sites of traditional craft work. Or take them to local museums. Discuss with them how what they see reflects the lives of the region's earlier inhabitants, and how lifestyles have changed in relation to the particular object you visit.

Visit a local kgotla, pitso, local/district council or law court. Ask students to discuss the following questions:

1. How does the settling of disputes reflect the composition of a community?

2. How can law be used to protect the poor as well as the powerful?

3. How are laws or customs enforced?

4. What is "justice", and how can a community make sure it is acted out?

Chapter 3:

Britain's Industrial Revolution

Feudal Society (53-54)

Make sure students understand these terms; "serfs"; "nobles"; "merchants", and "hierarchy".

Discuss the nature of inherited positions, and the powers which nobles had over serfs. Here are some points to include in discussions.

1.   Great chain of being: what does it mean to individuals to accept hierarchy as natural? Is it natural?

2.   Individuals' inability to change inherited status.

3.   Power of nobles over serfs' labour

4.   Freedom of towns (and merchants) compared to serfs, who were bound to land by law.

You may also want to discuss the way feudal society was imposed in Britain when William the Conqueror gave out land and power over serfs after his invasion in 1066. Compare feudal society to the traditional society in your area. How is it different? How might it be similar?

Scientific Method (A) (56)

Discuss the difference between the scientific method and other kinds of discoveries. Compare, for example, the process through which agricultural methods evolved over centuries through trial and error, and the scientific approach to agriculture shown during the "agricultural revolution" in the 1700s. Make sure students understand how hypotheses are developed, tested, and modified in scientific research.
You may want to invite a science teacher in to discuss the basic method of scientific research.

Scientific Method (B) (57)

Discuss how changes in technology lead to changes in productivity. Ask students to suggest examples of different technologies, and how these technologies can increase productivity.

Age of Exploration (54)

Ask students to suggest and discuss reasons for the age of exploration which preceded Europe's colonial adventures. Some reasons might include:

a)   the rise of long-distance trade after the Crusades;
b)   the rise of a cash economy, as people began to use money more, and to produce more for market;
c)   new interest in far-off places, and
d)   new technologies permitting further voyages, such as compasses, printing presses, maps, and new types of ships.

Background: Braudel, *Capitalism and Material Life, 1400-1600*

Voyages of Exploration

Divide students into small groups. Have each group research and report on the voyages of some of the more famous explorers of the 15th and 16th centuries, such as Magellan and Da Gama.

Role of the Printing Press (55)

Ask students to discuss what their world would be like if there were no printing presses. You may wish to consider:

a)   how many people would be able to read;
b)   how many people would get information;
c)   how it would limit people's ability to travel, trade and learn, and
d)   how it would affect scientific information.

Plunder

Discuss with students the plunder of Latin America by Spanish and

Portuguese conquistadors during the 16th and 17th centuries. You may
want to mention:

a)   the cultures which existed before the Spanish/Portuguese arrival
(Mayan, Aztec, Inca);

b)   the ways in which conquistadors used tricks and treaties to take
power;

c)   the decimation of the native Latin Americans, through war, disease
and forced labour;

d)   the division of Latin America by the Pope, and

e)   parallels to Southern Africa.

Technological Change (57-59, 59-60)

Ask students to research and report, singly or in small groups, on technological changes during Britain's industrial revolution in any of the following areas:

a)   navigational aids;
b)   metallurgy and mining;
c)   transportation and mining;
d)   forms of energy (water, steam, electricity).

Make sure reports consider questions such as:

a)   how the workforce is organised with different technologies;
b)   how much capital is required for different technologies, and
c)   how much raw material is needed for different technologies.

Enclosures (57)

Discuss with students the impact of the enclosure movement, in which self-
sufficient peasant families were evicted to make room for sheep, and later
for mechanised agriculture. Discuss the following issues.

1. Ownership of resources: why could some people take control of the land on which other people lived?

2. Demand of factories for raw materials such as wool: how is this linked to enclosures?

3. Increasing demand for food by a growing urban population.

4. The relation between changing agricultural techniques and changing organisation of production.

Discuss with students parallels to Southern Africa. You may wish to discuss South Africa's Land Act (1913) or the 1930 Land Apportionment Act in Southern Rhodesia..

Background: E.P. Thompson, *Making of the English Working Class*

Labour

Discuss with students the differences between these situations:

a) a craftsperson who own his own tools, or a cooperative which owns its tools and

b) a worker in a factory who works for someone else.

Points to consider:

a) who gets the 'profit' - the difference between the cost of making something and the price received;

b) who determines how much the person who actually produces the goods gets;

c) who controls how much, and what, is produced;

d) how much independence the worker has, and

e) how much control the worker has over how the product is used.

Unemployment (62, box)

Discuss the impact of high unemployment rates on wages, both during the industrial revolution in Britain and in your own country. Points to consider include:

a)   workers' ability to demand high wages;

b)   impact on government revenues when people have low incomes;

c)   problems for families when no one is working, and

d)   possibilities of resolving unemployment: should government set up special programmes to provide jobs? redistribute resources? promote cooperatives?

Triangle Trade (71-72)

Show students maps of the "triangular trade" between West Africa, the West Indies, and Britain. Discuss with students

a)   reasons for needing new sources of raw materials;

b)   reasons for needing slaves for plantations;

c)   reasons for taking slaves from Africa, and

d)   the use of manufactured goods to buy slaves in Africa.

Background: Rodney, *How Europe Underdeveloped Africa*
Slave Trade

Read students descriptions of the slave trade, either from Rodney's *How Europe Underdeveloped Africa*, or from Basil Davidson's *Black Mother*. Ask students to write stories, beginning in one of these ways:

a)   "One day I was working in the fields near our village, when suddenly..." (from the point of view of captured African), or

b) "We sailed into Benin harbour with a load of cloth and muskets, looking for a cargo of slaves for the West Indian plantations..." (from the point of view of a slave trader).

Read the best stories aloud to the class.

Impact of the Slave Trade   (68-71)

Discuss the impact of the slave trade on West African societies. You may wish to include:

a)   the "arms race", where people captured others to get guns to protect themselves;

b)   the loss of able-bodied people;

c)   the loss of skills, and

d)   increased dependence on imported manufactured goods.

Unions (72-74)

Invite a local labour officer or union representative to talk to students about his or her work in your community. Before the visitor comes, ask students to draw up a list of questions they wish to ask. Such questions might include the following.

a)   What is government policy toward unions?

b)   What unions exist locally?

c)   How are they organised?

d)   What activities do they undertake?

e)   What local union victories or defeats have occurred in the recent past?

UNIONS - Role Play

Divide students into groups of six, or have six students act out role-play before the rest of the class.

Roles:

MR MKATSHWA: representative from a pulp and paper workers union, which hopes to gain recognition as the representative of the 250 workers at the Paperco's Saw Mill, and seeks higher wages for the union members. The union threatens to call a strike if demands are not met.

MR MHLANGU: personnel official at the mill, who does not want the company to recognise the union.

MR KUNENE, MS NKOSI, MS HULELA: workers at the Paperco Mill. They have recently joined the union, and have asked the union representative to come to help them press for better wages and working conditions.

MR DLAMINI: Government labour officer who has been asked to arbitrate the situation.

Situation:

The 250 workers at the Paperco Sawmill have asked for a 15 cent an hour increase, and for recognition of the union as their legal representative in negotiations with management. They threaten to go on strike until their demands are met. The company - which would lose $250 a day if there was a strike - wants to avoid the strike, but also hopes to persuade workers not to join the union (for fear for future wage demands). The company offers a ten-cent-an-hour increase, and insists that higher increases will put Paperco out of business. However, Paperco will not allow workers to examine its books. The labour officer has been called in to arbitrate; the student playing the labour officer should try to follow your country's policy towards unions and strikes.

Points to consider:

1.   How much community support would a strike have? Would other workers be willing to replace strikers? How can this be avoided?

2.   How much unemployment is there in the area? Would workers risk losing their jobs if they join the union?

3.   How important is the product to the economy? Should that affect workers' decisions?

Progress

DEBATE: "ALTHOUGH TECHNOLOGICAL CHANGES MAY DIS-
TURB PEOPLE'S LIVES, ECONOMIC GROWTH ULTIMATELY
BENEFITS EVERYONE"

Points to consider include those listed below.

Pro

- Any growth may temporarily disturb people's lives, but ultimately it brings benefit;

- People must learn to adapt to new conditions;

- People must take advantage of scientific changes;

Con

- Technological change should take account of people;

- Growth alone is not important, what matters is how increased productivity is used;

- Changes in productivity often benefit one group, not everyone.

FIELD TRIPS

Take students to see one or several industrial processes. Before they go, have students draw up a list of questions such as those below.

1. What is produced?

2. What raw materials are used?

3. How do industrial processes differ from traditional ways of making goods?

4. What fuel source is used?

5. Who owns and manges the factory?

6. Where do workers come from?

7. What kind of capital is needed to set up the factory?

8. How are production decisions made?

9. Who buys the product?

Note: In Chapter I's classroom activities (see above) a very similar Field Trip was suggested in the section on development strategies. Teachers may wish to omit this second trip or combine the two.

Chapter 4: Imperialism in Southern Africa

Colonial Rule (A)

Discuss with students the early arrival of colonial settlers. The following are some points to consider.

1.   What do the boxes on Rhodes and Kipling (pp 79 and 80) reveal about the motives of 19th century imperialists?

2.   How was colonial rule imposed in your region (treaties, concessions, battles, etc.)?

3.   Looking at maps showing expansion of colonial rule in Southern Africa (e.g. 1652, 1820, 1880 and 1900), what can students see about how the expansion of colonial rule corresponded with the discovery of mineral deposits?

Make sure students understand the term "imperialism".

Colonial Rule (B)

Look at the early imposition of colonial rule in your area. Some points to consider:

a)   motives of early white arrivals;
b)   methods of taking control (treaties, battles, etc.);
c)   methods of enforcing rule (through local leaders; through force); and
d)   the response of local people to colonial rule (ask students if they know of any local resistance to colonial rule).

Concessions

DEBATE: "SOUTHERN AFRICAN RULERS IN THE MID 19TH CENTURY WERE WISER TO SELL CONCESSIONS BUT RETAIN POLITICAL CONTROL, THAN TO TRY TO FIGHT, AND RISK LOSING EVERYTHING.

You may want to state this debate in more concrete terms, by comparing two leaders with different approaches such as Swaziland's Mbandzeni and the Ndebele's Lobengula.

Pro
- Colonial invaders had more modern weapons, and would win anyway.

- By keeping political control, the people were unified under their own ruler, rather than having to accept new administrative units.

Con
- Rulers couldn't be sure they would lose if they fough
- Political control may be meaningless if you make so many concessions.
- Concessions only satisfied the colonial rulers when no settlers wanted the land.

Imperialism

Discuss the difference between direct and indirect rule. Here are some issues to raise with class.

1. Why are settlers likely to use direct rule?
2. Why was indirect rule more common in West Africa, and direct rule more common in Southern Africa?
3. What were the advantages and disadvantages of each method to colonial administrations?
4. What were the advantages and disadvantages of each method to the local people?
5. Why was direct rule often more costly?

Imperialism Today

If you can get information on current imperialist efforts, you may wish to spend a lesson comparing modern "imperialism" to 19th century European colonial ventures. For example, in 1983, you might have looked at the United States invasion of Grenada, and discussed the general problems in Central America. Some of the issues you might have pointed out to students include:

a)   the way in which the United States interfered with democratic processes in Grenada (compare this to British colonial attitudes in Southern Africa at the turn of the century);

b)   what the United States might have hoped to gain from its invasion (compare this to 19th century motives for colonialism);

c)   the US failure to declare Grenada a "colony" (how has the world view of colonial ventures changed in the last 70 years?); and

d)   current struggles against imperialism around the world (where are such movements, why have they grown up, what are their demands?).

Colonial Rule (C)

Discuss the problems of imposing law on a completely different culture. Ask students if they can imagine any difficulties that colonial rulers in Southern Africa might have faced, such as:

a) differences in views of land ownership;
b) differences in family structure;
c) differences in powers of chiefs over subjects; and
d) different religious beliefs.

Resistance to Colonial Rule

Discuss examples of local resistance to colonial rule, including both early resistance and later attempts to regain independence. Some issues to discuss would be:

a)   early resistance in your area;
b)   other forms of resistance than military (through churches, protest campaigns, etc.); and
c)   political resistance (history of local political parties, etc).

Cash Economy

As a class, try to find examples of the arrival of a cash economy in your area.

a)   Have students list several common items around the house.
b)   Have students list sources of these items for four generations, and fill in a table like the one on page 73.

Look at the different kinds of "wants" people of different generations have had. For example, the class might try to list the "wants" of their grandparents, and of themselves;
-Grandparents: cattle, fields, hoes...
-Students: education, jobs, car...
Discuss the differences between the generations, and how these might reflect the changes in society as a whole.

Migrant Labour (A) (90-91)

Discuss the rise of the migrant labour system in your area, and how it must have affected people in the past. Some points to raise include:
a) motives of the early migrant labourers;
b) motives of mine-owners to use migrant labourers;
c) impact on families; and
d) impact on local productivity.
Background: L. Callinicos, *Gold and Workers*

Migrant Labour (B)

Have students (singly or in small groups) interview returned migrants in your community. Students should make up lists of questions before they go to interview, and then report back to the class. Below are some questions which might be included.

1) Why did the person go?

2) What kind of work did he or she find?
3) How did the worker find the job?
4) What were the conditions like?
5) How did it affect the family at home?
6) How much money could the worker send back home?
7) How long did the worker stay away?

Figure 5

Items	Great Grand parents	Grand parents	Parents	Self
Pots	(Home-made)			
Method of Transport		(Train)		
Food			(Commercially grown & sold)	

Look at the different kinds of 'Wants' people of different generations have had.

MIGRANT LABOUR IN LESOTHO -
Simulation Game

Role Cards

MR LENKA:
A young married man, who has passed standard six, wants to go and work in the mines of South Africa because he is not employed in Lesotho.

MR SELLO:
A migrant worker who has recently come back home. He tells his friends why it is important to work in the mines of South Africa, i.e. he has learnt to repair machinery.

MR BONVA:
A rich man who has built a beautiful house and educated his children through the help of money earned from the mines of South Africa. In addition to what Mr Sello has said he explains how he has achieved a higher standard of living for his family.

MS LENTO:
She has nine children. Her husband works in the mines. She is responsible for the her home, fields and children. She complains that her husband does not write her letters. He does not send money to support the family. As a result the family suffers from starvation. She is now engaged in brewing beer to make money.

MS LENTO'S SON LOLO:
He does not attend school, due to the fact that there is no money for uniform and school-fees. His duty is to look after the cattle because there is no herdboy in his family.

MS LERATO:
A woman who has built a shebeen in Mohale's Hoek district. She awaits the young men from the mines. She explains how she makes money through them before they get back home.

MR MPOPO:

He comes from the mines at Welkom. He tells his wife that he has lost all the money he had (M500.00) at Mrs Lerato's shebeen. He was drunk.

MS MPOPO:

She is very angry and thinks it is better to divorce her husband as he does not help her to support the family.

MR BABO:

As a mine worker, he complains that he does not understand why part of his salary is taken by the government.

THE MINISTER OF AGRICULTURE:

He explains the bad effects of the migrant labour system on agriculture. The strong able-bodied men leave farming in the hands of women and boys who do not know modern farming techniques. As a result there is low productivity and the produce is not enough to satisfy the needs of the people in the country.

THE MINISTER OF FINANCE:

He suggests that part of the salaries of the people who work in the mines should be saved in the Lesotho Bank so as to contribute towards the development of the country. Through deferred payments the Government will be able to build projects. The migrant workers will be able to withdraw it when they get back home.

THE MINISTER OF EDUCATION:

He is anxious to change the system of education. It is better to introduce technical or practical subjects like Development Studies which will equip the students with necessary skills. By so doing, they will be prepared for the world of work. They will be able to mobilise their own resources in order to satisfy their needs rather than go and seek jobs and develop the Republic of South Africa. The government is capable of employing the people of higher educational qualifications only, e.g. those with C.O.S.C., S.T.C. or University degree. People can be trained better by non-formal technical training on the job.

THE PRIME MINISTER:

He suggests that more jobs should be created in the rural areas so as to reduce the number of young able-bodied men who work in the mines because the migrant labour system retards development in the country.

The Structure of the Simulation

There are thirteen cards in the simulation game (The teacher can invent more cards so as to include more pupils). On each card is written a name and what he or she is expected to do in the game. Let the students choose the roles they would like to play. The teacher gives each student a copy of the sheet on "Advantages and disadvantages of the migrant labour system in Lesotho" a week before they play the game. By so doing she will help them read and have an idea of what they are expected to do. Let the students collect information by interviewing their parents or relatives at home.

The teacher divides the students into two groups. One group of students represents the villagers in their casual meeting and another group represents the ministers in parliamentary session. They have name labels to identify them.

SCENE I

Group 1 consists of the following villagers:

Mr Mpopo, Mr Sello, Mr Bonva, Mrs Lerato, Mr Lenka, Mr Babo, Ms Lento's son and Mrs Mpopo

They sit in a circle and discuss the bad and good effects of the migrant labour system in Lesotho, how it retards development in their families, and how it has improved their standard of living.

SCENE II

Group II represents the Ministers of Finance, Agriculture and Education, and the Prime Minister. They all sit around the table for the parliamentary session. The rest of the class represents the members of the parliament. They discuss possible solutions to the

problems of the migrant labour system.
All the students are given a chance to argue their points, so as to make the simulation game more interesting.

SCENE III

The Prime Minister holds a general meeting in the village. He explains to them how the migrant labour system has retarded development in Lesotho. He suggests possible solutions and the other ministers support him, that is, they give suggestions of what should be done in order to reduce the number of migrants. The villagers are allowed to ask questions or to suggest possible solutions.

Follow up:

1.   Group Work

The teacher divides the class into groups of five. The students discuss the advantages and disadvantages of the migrant labour system. Each group chooses the secretary who writes the points and the chairman who should present the group's report.

2.   Assignment

The students should write an essay on the advantages and disadvantages of the migrant labour system.

Information Sheet: "The Migrant Labour System"

Advantages

-Since Lesotho faces a social problem of unemployment, most men flock to the mines of South Africa to seek jobs. In this case men are determined to work for money to satisfy the needs of their families.

-The migrant brings home money to satisfy their basic needs, namely food, shelter, and clothes. By so doing, the standard of living rises.

They send their children to school and educate them.

-Some migrant workers are taught how to read and write and others are given a chance to learn technical skills. Sometimes they can use these skills in Lesotho when they return home.

-The deferred payments of the migrants are saved and deposited in the Lesotho Bank. This money can be used for short-term investment in Lesotho, that is, it is lent out to people who want to build projects of various kinds. In this way, the migrants' savings contribute towards the development of the country. Migrants are free to withdraw their money from the Bank when they come home.

Disadvantages

-Migrant labour puts a big strain on family life. Men leave their wives behind and the wives have to take responsibility for looking after the home, the fields and the children.

-Farming suffers because it is left in the hands of women, young boys and old men. This is one reason that Lesotho does not produce enough food for its people.

-The migrant labour system strengthens South Africa and makes Lesotho more dependent and vulnerable.

Acknowledgement: Lintle Pheko, National University of Lesotho, 1983

Urbanisation (A): The Informal Sector (91-92)

Discuss the problems of rapid urbanisation with students. Then have students, in groups or in pairs, interview local "informal sector" workers. Draw up a list of questions, such as the following.

1. What does the worker do?
2. What tools are needed?
3. How did the worker get the tools?
4. What raw materials are needed?
5. How does the worker get raw materials?
6. How much does the worker earn per hour?
7. How many people in the area do the same sort of thing?
8. What are the advantages and disadvantages of this work?
9. Would the worker prefer a formal sector job?

Discuss the responses in class.

Urbanisation (B)

Using housing survey (see above in the Chapter on Changing Societies), discuss:

a) problems of urbanisation in your community;
b) reasons for rapid urbanisation in your area;
c) impact on rural areas;
d) impact on towns; and
e) possible solutions to problems such as unemployment and lack of social services.

Population Growth (A) (92-93)

On the board, show students how population grows. Draw a "family tree":

Have students draw their own family trees as far as they can. Count the number of people in each generation. What does this tree show them?

Population Growth (B)

Using your country's most recent census, draw your country's age pyramid (showing how many people are in each group). It should look something like the example on the page opposite.

Discuss with students:

a) the proportion of the population under 15;
b) the reasons for this "shape" in the population;
c) possible effects of this "shape"; and
d) ways of dealing with rapid population growth.

Education (A)

Sir Seretse Khama, then president of Botswana, said in 1970:

"We were taught, sometimes in a very positive way, to despise ourselves and our ways of life. We were made to believe that we had no past to speak of, no history to boast of. The past, so far as we were concerned, was just a blank and nothing more. Only the present mattered and we had very little control over it..."

Discuss this comment with students. What does it say about the imposition of European culture in Southern Africa? What impact might this have had on racial stereotypes? On African societies? Is it true today? Perhaps you could ask students to write essays discussing the quote.

Education (B)

Have students try to find out about your school's history. When was it founded? Why? Who built it? How was the curriculum set? In what ways was the community involved?

Education (C)

DEBATE: "SCHOOLS IN SOUTHERN AFRICA SHOULD NOT IMITATE EUROPEAN SCHOOLS, BUT SHOULD TRY TO DEVELOOP CURRICULA WHICH ARE RELEVANT TO STUDENTS' LIVES".

Figure 6

Years of age:

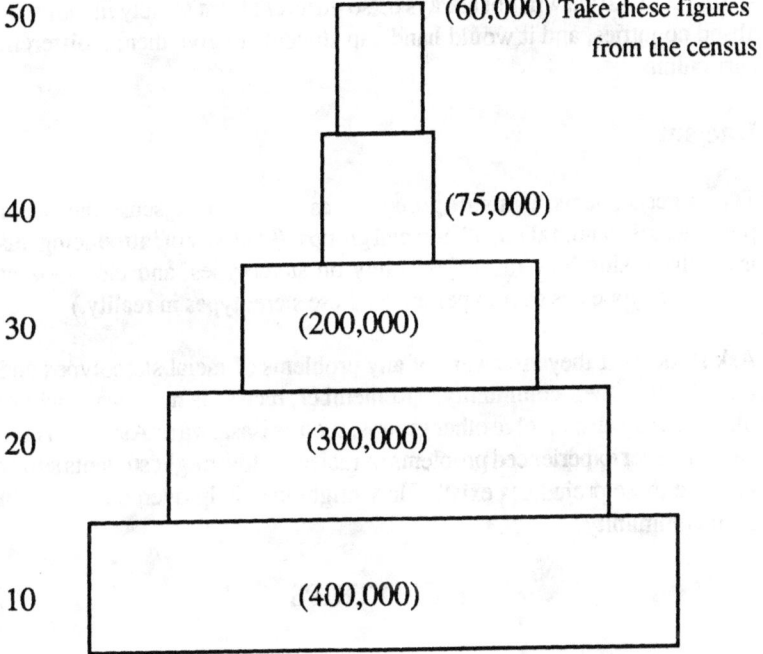

50   (60,000) Take these figures
                                from the census

40   (75,000)

30   (200,000)

20   (300,000)

10   (400,000)

Pro

- Students should learn about their own culture and history
- Students should learn things that are appropriate to their lives, not subjects designed for life in European societies.
- Students can only participate in development if they understand the real situation in which they live.

Con

- The world is increasingly small, and people everywhere need the same basic analytic tools.
- Students in Southern Africa need to be able to cope with "modern" society, and they need to study "modern" subjects to do so
- Southern Africa will not always be so different from society in industrialised countries, and it would handicap students to give them a different curriculum

Racism

Try to get students, in small groups or as a class, to discuss the racial prejudices they hold about other racial groups. (One way of introducing this is by discussing how racial jokes rely on stereotypes, and then look at whether anyone has ever experienced these stereotypes in reality.)

Ask students if they are aware of any problems of racial stereotypes and prejudices in their community. (Remember, racism is not always white/ black: it may also involve other groups, such as Basarwa or Asians.) Have students ever experienced problems of racism? How might students suffer because these prejudices exist? How might they help overcome them in their community?

FIELD TRIPS

If there are any sites of resistance to colonialism near you, you might take students to view one such symbol of their national heritage. For example, in Lesotho students should visit Thaba Basiu, to gain a greater understanding of Moshoeshoe's importance.

In Zimbabwe, students could visit the Matopos site of Rhodes' negotiations with the Ndebele.

In most parts of Southern Africa there are places nearby which mark some important event of national resistance and pride.

Chapter Five: Government's Role in Development

Independence (101-104)

Make sure students are familiar with the struggle for independence in your country, and the process by which it was achieved. Points to discuss include:

a) resistance to colonial rule;
b) efforts to negotiate independence, and
c) armed struggle (if any)

You many wish to compare differences between the struggle for independence in your country and in other areas; for example, if your country was able to negotiate independence easily, compare and contrast that process to the struggle in Zimbabwe.

Background: Parsons, N.A. *New History of Southern Africa* and Martin, D. and Johnson, P., *The Struggle for Zimbabwe*

Types of Government (102-103)

Discuss with students the differences between:

a) chiefly rule;
b) direct democracy, and
c) representative democracy

Ask students which they would prefer, and why. Which is most suitable for different types of communities - schools, towns, nations, etc? Why? In small groups, have students list the advantages and disadvantages of each type of government, and discuss which type of government seems most appropriate for their country.

Constitution (A) (103, box)

Give students copies of your country's constitution. Discuss the following with them:

a) the method of choosing or peacefully changing rulers in the constitution;
b) the role of the civil service according to the constitution;
c) the powers of and constraints on the government, and
d) the role of the courts in restraining government

Discuss with students the problems that might exist in making sure the constitution is followed. How should countries avoid corruption in government? What happens if a government refuses to hold elections? How might the constitution be made more appropriate to your country's culture and traditions?

Constitution (B)

As a class, try drawing up a constitution for your school. The constitution should include the following points:

1   How the headmaster is appointed. Who appoints and who is consulted?
2.   How the headmaster's power may be limited. To whom can students and staff appeal? How can the headmaster be removed?
3   How staff is appointed.
4.   Powers of and possible checks on teachers. (To whom can students appeal? How can teachers be removed?)
5   Possible student representation in school decisions. How should student representatives be chosen? How can they advise on school policy? What checks might exist on student representatives' powers?
6   What links should exist between community and school? How can community representatives be chosen? How can they advise on school policy? What are community representatives' powers?

Army and Police

DEBATE: "EVERY COUNTRY SHOULD HAVE A STRONG STAND-

ING ARMY, AND YOUTHS SHOULD BE REQUIRED TO SPEND TWO YEARS DOING NATIONAL SERVICE."

Pro

- The army can protect against invasions.
- National service builds a sense of national unity.
- The army and police can defend the legal order within the country.

Con

- A large army is expensive; developing countries have more important ways of spending scarce resources.
- A large army can overthrow the government, and take power illegally.
- Instead of military national service, youths should spend two years working to develop the country

Taxes (108, box)

What taxes are paid in your country? Discuss with students your government's policy on the following issues.

1. Income tax: is it designed to take more from wealthy people, or is everyone taxed equally on their income?
2. General sales taxes: do people pay sales taxes on all goods? What different kinds of impact might this have on poor people and wealthy ones? Is this the fairest way to raise government revenue?
3. Luxury sales tax: are some goods - such as tobacco, liquor and petrol-specially taxed? What different impact does this have on rich and poor people? How might it affect what people buy?
4. Licences: what kinds of licences must people buy (for example, drivers, hunting, radio, or to sell liquor)? Do licences limit people's activities? Does it raise very much revenue? Are all licenses designed for the same purposes?
5. What are some other government revenue-raising projects (e.g. a new hotel, a state lottery, nationalised companies)?
You can probably find out about the tax system from the national budget or from representatives from the ministry of finance and planning.

Infrastructure (109, box)

Display a map of your country's roads and railroads. Discuss with the class the questions below.

1. How does infrastructure favour economic growth in certain areas?
2. How is production in certain areas helped by a developed infrastructure?
3. Who decided where roads and railways should go? Who decides where new ones should go?
4. Which areas should get high priorities today?

Development Banks (110)

Ask a representative from your country's development or national bank to tell the class about its lending policy. Before the bank representative comes, ask students to draw up a list of questions to ask, such as the following.

1. How can people apply for loans?
2. What are interest rates, compared to commercial interest rates?
3. How are interest rates set?
4. Who is given loans - are special groups favoured? special products?
5. What collateral is needed?
6. How does the development bank fit in with the development strategy of the country?

Parastatals (110)

Tell students about those industries or enterprises your government owns or runs directly. If possible, have a representative from a parastatal come to talk to your class. Some of the issues to raise might include the following.

1. Why did the government get involved in those particular enterprises?
2. How does the activity benefit the government? The country?
3. What problems might there be in the parastatal?

Education Policy (111-113)

Ask your headmaster or a representative from the ministry of-education to discuss your government's educational policy with the class. Before the headmaster or representative comes, have students draw up a list of questions they would like answered. Questions might include:

a) policy concerning building new schools;
b) policy during the colonial era toward education;
c) policy toward non-formal education;
d) policy toward adult education;
e) efforts to revise curriculum, and
f) efforts to include practical subjects and vocational training in schools.

Education

DEBATE: "IT IS BETTER TO PROVIDE UNIVERSAL PRIMARY EDUCATION THAN TO PUT SCARCE RESOURCES INTO BUILD-ING MORE SECONDARY SCHOOLS".

Pro

-Primary education is suitable preparation for most types of work
-Scarce resources should be equally shared out; further education can come when everyone has had basic education
-People can find other ways than school of furthering learning, once they have achieved basic literacy.

Con

-Concentrating on primary education will perpetuate the lack of skills in many developing countries
-Countries need more educated people to run things
- It is better to have a few people with high levels of skills than to have many people with lower skills.
- In order to have primary schools, countries need higher schools to train teachers.

Health Services (A) (113-114)

Ask a local health officer to visit your class. Have students draw up a list of questions to be answered during the visit, such as:

89

a) major health problems in the area such as nutrition, chronic diseases, housing and water;
b) government policies for dealing with problems, and
c) what students might do help improve the level of health in their community.

Health Services (B)

DEBATE: "GOVERNMENT SHOULD INVEST MORE IN PRIMARY HEALTH CARE THAN IN TRYING TO CURE DISEASES"

Pro

-Preventitive health care prevents the diseases in the first place
-Primary health care reaches more people
-Later, hospitals can be built; the first step is to raise the general level of health

Con

-It's often hard to change people's lifestyles to prevent disease.
-It's hard to get primary health information to rural areas, and anyway poor people often can't afford many of the ways in which they could improve health.
-No matter how much health information is available, people will still get some diseases.

Point out to students that primary and secondary health policies are not exclusive; most governments find some mix of the two. The question is what the mix should be.

Budget

Show students your country's budget (you can usually find a newspaper article summarising important aspects of the budget). Ask students the questions below:

1) Where will government revenues come from?
2) Which ministries seem to have highest priority? Why?

3) Which ministries have small budgets? Why?
4) Do students think this is the wisest allocation of resources? Why or why not?

Development Plan (115-118)

Look at your country's development plan. Ask students to discuss the following issues.

1) What are the plan's goals?
2) What is the government doing to promote economic growth?
3) How is it trying to share benefits of economic growth between the people?
4) How will the government spend its revenues?
5) What kinds of production will it try to promote?
6) What kind of education policy is being followed?
7) What kind of health care policy is included in the plan?
8) What foreign aid is being sought? For what kind of projects? From which countries? Why?
9) What do students think the plan will achieve?
10)What efforts did the government make to discuss the plan with the people?

FOREIGN AID - Simulation Game

"CALLING ON THE U.N. AGENCIES FOR HELP"

Objectives

1.   Students will be able to give the functions of: U.N.E.S.C.O., W.H.O., F.A.O. and I.L.O. and say what the initials stand for.

2.   Students will be able to identify common problems in Third World countries, and say which U.N. agencies can provide help to solve such problems.

3.   Students will lpractise formulating development plans, solving problems, and taking decisions.

4.   Students will appreciate the work of the U.N. agencies in development.

Resources Needed

1   Materials about the U.N. and its agencies: maps, pamphlets, books, magazines and case-studies of how the U.N. helped different countries can be obtained from the U.N. Information Centre in your capital.

2.   Questions and answers for the groups to use (see below).

3.   Wall-charts about the four agencies (see below)

4.   Cards showing types of aid (see below)

Questions and Answers These should be written or typed out, each on a separate strip of paper. The strips must be carefully numbered. The strips are shared out among the members of the grouup. They read them out, thus acting a discussion.

GROUP A

Qu. 1.
When one walks in our streets, one sees girls, boys, women and men going about dirty, ragged, hungry. What is the cause of this?

Ans. 1.
There are no jobs for them. They have nowhere to get money.

Qu. 2. How can we solve this problem?

Ans. 2. We must put them to work making things out of our raw materials.

Qu. 3. Well, we have forests and cattle, we grow cotton and coconuts. But we do not have the right machines for making furniture and shoes, or for weaving. Where can we get them?

Ans. 3. Perhaps the United Nations can advise us.

Qu. 4. What use are machines? Our poor people are not trained to use complicated machinery. How can they be trained?

Ans. 4. Go and find out which agency of the Untied Nations can offer us help.

GROUP B

Qu. 1. I hear that our food supplies are running low. This year the farmers have not produced enough grain for our people. Why is their productivity so low?

Ans. 1. The soil is exhausted. The farmers do not know how to improve the land. They have old-fashioned tools and use poor seed.

Qus. 2. What can we do in this situation?

Ans. 2. We could ask other countries to send us Food Aid.

Qu. 3. That would only feed us for a season . How can we improve our whole agricultural sector?

Ans. 3. Our farmers need advice and training.

Qu. 4. But we have too few agricultural extension workers and they are badly trained. Where can we get more expert help?

Ans. 4. Go and find out which agency of the United Nations can help us.

GROUP C

Qu. 1. Most of our JC students failed their science exams last year. What is the cause of this?

Ans. 1. The country doesn't have enough science teachers, laboratories or science equipment.

Qu. 2. Some of the Std. 7 leavers did not get places in our High Schools. There are many boys and girls idling at home or thieving on the streets. Why are they not in school?

Ans. 2. It is clear that we do not have enough secondary schools, especially technical and vocational schools.

Qu. 3. We must quickly build more schools. But where can we find teachers?

Ans. 3. We must bring them from other countries until we have trained our own.

Qu. 4. How can we make sure we get good teachers who will understand our needs?

Ans. 4. Let us ask the correct agency of the United Nations for advice.

GROUP D

Qu. 1. Cholera! We do not have enough medicines, and we have few doctors. What can we do?

Ans. 1. Our traditional healers will deal with this sickness.

Qu. 2. They cannot cure cholera. They don't have the right medicine. People are dying. What else can you suggest?

Ans. 2. We don't have money, there's nothing we can do. Let us pray.

Qu. 3. This thing is serious. Who can we turn to?

Ans. 3. The United Nations can perhaps help.

Qu. 4. What kind of help can they give us in this emergency?

Ans. 4. Let us go to their offices and find out.

Wall-Charts: These should be large, with writing large enough to be read across the room. They could be illustrated with pictures cut out from UN materials.

International Labour Organisation (ILO)

1. Improves working and living conditions of workers.

2. Creates jobs.

3. Trains workers etc.

Food and Agricultural Organisation (FAO)

1. Improves production and distribution of food

2. Fights animal and plant diseases.

3. Educates farmers.

4. Overcomes waste of land through erosion etc.

United Nations Educational Scientific and Cultural Organisation (UNESCO)

1. Improves education

2. Promotes culture

3. Trains people in different educational sectors. etc.

World Health Organisation (WHO)

1. Improves the health of people.

2. Plans health projects

3. Trains health workers etc

More details of their aims and work can be added.

Cards: These should be large enough to show several types of aid that are to be given by each agency. They carry the agency heading, and are pinned on the wall beside the big charts.

Examples:

ILO
1. $190 million loan
2. $60 million grant
3. Training for 9 workers
4. Shoe factory machinery

FAO
1. Emergency food supplies
2. $286 million soft loan
3. Pesticides and fertilisers
4. 3 expert trainers of farmers

UNESCO
1. 9 Science teachers
2. $60 million grant
3. 6 scholarships for educators
4. School science equipment

WHO
1. $50 million worth of drugs
2. 9 trained doctors
3. 20 scholarships for nurses
4. An operating theatre

Preparation

1. Wall-charts and cards are stuck up on the walls, together with appropriate maps and posters from the UN.

2. Furniture is arranged so that students can work in 4 groups of 8-10.

3. On the table for each group is placed:

-a large label with the name of a country;
-books, pictures, maps, articles etc. about that country and its needs and
-one bundle of strips of "questions and answers".

*(**N.B.** Choose names of countries for which you have good materials. When this game was tested, the following were used: Lesotho, Botswana, India and Brazil. Make sure the "questions and answers" dialogue is roughly accurate for the country concerned!)*

Method of Playing

1. Students are given 5 minutes to look at the wall-charts, cards and posters.

2. Students are divided into equal groups, and sit down at the tables. They choose a chairman and secretary.

3. Teacher informs them that they are the "Cabinet Ministers" of their country.

4. They are given 5-10 minutes to read the materials to learn about "their" country. (*NB This stage could be done in a previous lesson, either by teaching the whole class about each country, or dividing them into the groups and letting them do their own research*).

5. Teacher gives them instructions for the rest of the game.

-Share out the strips of paper, and then read the dialogue in order i.e. Question 1, Answer 1, Question 2, and so on.

-Discuss which Agency is appropriate. When they have decided, the whole group may go to the correct wall chart, and find out what aid is available.

-The group then returns to their table and discusses which of the types of aid they most need. They may only choose two.

-The group secretary writes the report, saying which two types of aid they want, and why they have chosen these.

6. If there is time, the teacher may call for a 2-minute break, and then move all the groups round to a different table. The procedure is then repeated, each group studying a different country and seeking aid from a different agency.

7. Each group presents its report (or two reports if there was time for a repeat) to the whole class.

Comments

This could be used to introduce the topic of the UN agencies.

As follow-up, a speaker or a film on the work of the agencies could be used. It is likely that local examples of UN agency work can be found.

The most valuable part of the exercise is the group discussions about which types of aid are most useful and why. This stage should not be hurried. The teacher can listen in, and note good points for later discussion with the whole class.

Ensure that all groups have learnt something about each agency; it may be sufficient to leave the wall displays for a few days, and give a short test on the information afterwards.

Although this simulation will take the teacher some time to prepare, all the materials and charts can be stored and used over and over again.

Acknowledgement: Mrs. G.M. Lehloenya,
Development Studies Ideas Book, 1983

FIELD TRIPS

Take students to watch local government in process. If possible, take them to see a parliamentary debate. If the national centre is too far, take them to watch a discussion at local level, in Kgotla, pitso or municipal or district council offices. Afterwards, discuss the following questions.

1. Which issues seemed important during the debate?
2. What decisions faced the government/council?
3. How were the decisions made?
4. How were they to be enforced?

Chapter 6: International Trade

Exports (124-133)

Give students a list of your country's main export products (if possible, include the value of each product, so that students can discuss which export products earn the most for your country).

Discuss, as class or in small groups the questions below.

1. Which export products are most important for your country?
2. Which export products are primary products? Where are they processed?
3. What are export products used for? What else might the same products be used for?
4. Where are most of the export goods sold? Where are they refined or used?
5. Where else in the world are the same goods produced?
6. What resources go into producing these export goods? What else might the same resources be used for?

Imports (A)

Give students a list of the main goods imported to your country. Discuss with students the following issues.

1. What kinds of goods are imported - manufactured goods, food, light consumer goods, and/or heavy industrial products?
2. Who uses them - individuals, industries, rich people, or poor people?
3. What kinds of controls does the government try to place on imports? Do these controls work? What are they supposed to do?
4. Could these goods be produced locally? Why aren't they? What resources, including skills and machines, would be needed to produce them?

TRADE - Simulation Game

This game is intended to help the players understand more clearly how trade can affect the prosperity of a country. Our planet is divided: the northern industrialised countries such as North America, Europe or Japan have a much higher standard of living than the countries in Latin America, Africa or Asia. There are many ways of explaining this difference, but it is certain that the gap between rich and poor is maintained and even made wider by a world trading system that helps the strong, well-organised countries rather than the poorer ones. This game tries to show how trading actually works: who benefits and who loses. But one of its aims is to make clear the basic issues that determine these relationships.

The game is designed to illustrate how the process of trade can benefit and hinder the economic development of different communities or countries. It aims to generate interest and discussion about the world trading system in an enjoyable and non-academic way: discussions on trade could be extremely boring but the players will almost certainly want to talk about their experiences during the playing of the game and this in turn should lead to a broader discussion about trading relationships.

You need at least one hour for the game and discussion; with a well informed group allow longer - up to one and a half hours.

Playing the Game

Accommodation and Furniture

You need a room large enough to accommodate up to six groups of four to six players each; leave plenty of circulation space between the groups. Most classrooms are just about large enough if the desks or tables can be moved around, but ideally if you have a group of 30 it would be better to use a small hall.

The organisers need a table or desk, and a blackboard or uncluttered wall surface for sticking up posters.

Even if the number of players is smaller than 30, e.g. 15 - 20, there should always be at least five different groups and at least one group should have a Grade A resource set.

Each of the six groups needs a table or desk as a work surface and a chair or two for each group would be useful.

For 30 players you will require this equipment:

30 A4 sheets of paper - plain and all the same colour
30 "pound notes" of £100 each
2 sheets of coloured sticky paper
4 pairs of scissors
4 rulers
2 compasses for drawing circles
2 set squares
2 protractors
14 lead pencils
2 diagrams of shapes (see next page)

In addition it is useful to have some extra pencils and paper similar to the original 30 sheets for "emergencies" as well as some paper for the organiser to use for passing messages.

Preparation

All the players need to be able to see the Diagram of Shapes during the game, so this needs to be copied on to a blackboard or made into a poster for displays. Depending on the shape of your room you may need two posters.

The equipment indicated above needs to be arranged into "Resource Sets" as shown below:

Grade A - two sets of the following:

2 pairs of scissors
2 rulers
1 compass
1 set square

Figure 7: Diagram of Shapes

All edges must be cut with scissors

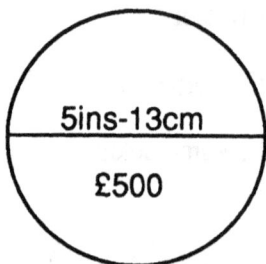

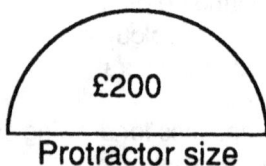

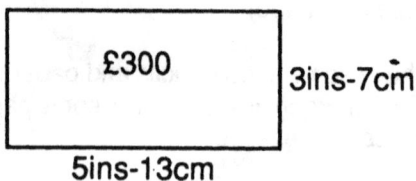

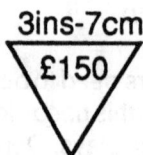

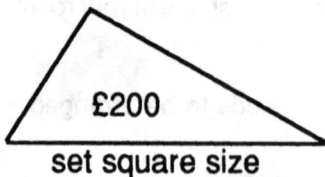

5ins-13cm

£500

£200

Protractor size

£300

3ins-7cm

5ins-13cm

3ins-7cm

£150

£200

set square size

Scale: |4cm|

Suggested dimensions - adopt either inches or cm, not both

1 protractor
1 sheet of paper
6 "pound notes"
4 lead pencils

Grade B - two sets of the following:

10 sheets of paper
1 sheet sticky paper
2 "pound notes"

Grade C - two sets of the following:

4 sheets of paper
2 "pound notes"
2 pencils

The furniture of the room needs to be arranged so that there are six areas for the groups to work from: each area should have a flat working surface.

You need two organisers per game: one to act as banker and one to act as leader. The leader's role is to keep control of the entire game, taking note of how it develops and occasionally changing the game's direction by introducing new elements into it. Leaders must be ready to lead the discussion at the end of the game. For this it is useful to jot down anything interesting or significant that players have said or done during the game.

The banker requires a pen or pencil and a sheet of paper with six columns - one for each of the six groups.

With the Diagram of Shapes in position, the equipment arranged in sets, the banker's sheet prepared and the furniture rearranged you are now ready to play the game.

Leader's Instructions

1. Split the players into five or six groups as shown, allocate each group an area in the room or hall and then give each group a set of materials as indicated.

RESOURCE-SET	SOME SUGGESTED COUNTRY NAMES FOR GROUPS
Grade A	USA or UK
Grade A	Italy or France
Grade B	India or Brazil
Grade B	Nigeria or Peru
Grade C	Tanzania or Kenya
Grade C	Burma or Ghana

Do not point out the groups that they are receiving different sets of materials; they will notice soon enough.

2. Now read out the objectives and rules of the game to the players. These are as follows:

"The objective of each group is to make as much wealth for itself as possible by using the materials given to it. No other materials can be used. The wealth is made by manufacturing paper shapes. The goods you are going to manufacture are the shapes shown on the Diagram of Shapes. Each shape has its own value as shown on the Diagram and these paper shapes are given to the banker in batches for checking and crediting to your bank account. You can manufacture as many shapes as you like - the more you make the wealthier you will be.

"There are just four simple rules:

a) All the shapes need to be cut with clean sharp edges using scissors and must be of the exact size shown - the shapes are taken to the banker for your account.

b) You can only use the materials that have been given out.

c) There is to be no physical force used during the game.

d) The leader represents the United Nations and will intervene in any disagreement".

Repeat the rules quickly and then announce that "manufacturing can begin".

3. At the beginning of the game some confused or puzzled players will bombard you with questions: Can we borrow scissors? Where can I get scissors? Can we trade? Why haven't we got scissors (paper etc.)? What's the sticky paper for?

Resist all temptation to answer these questions - just repeat the rules or stay silent.

After a difficult minute or two of confusion at the beginning, the players will start moving around the room and begin trading; the initiative should come from them, not you.

4. The manufacturing and trading should continue for about 30 - 45 minutes depending on the size and interest of the group.

Points for the leader during and after the Game

A. Watch what is happening!

The Grade A groups will begin making shapes as soon as they have all the materials and equipment, but they will soon run short of raw materials and probably try to buy some paper from other groups. At first the groups with paper will probably sell it for a very low price. Note how the "terms of trade" change during the game and point this out later. You will be the only person who can see how the game is developing as a whole; the players will be engrossed in their own groups so it is important for you to note the types of alliances and deals which develop and bring these into the discussion at the end.

B. Stimulate activity!

Some groups will feel impotent and neglected. In order to encourage trading activity, the leader may have to feed in more information and create new situations which have parallels in the real world. Some suggestions are made below (see F). Some of these changes will apply to all the groups, but others will be communicated by secret messages given to particular groups only by the leader.

C. Changing market values

After a while, change the value of some of the shapes, so that, for example, rich groups find that their compasses are no longer as useful as they were for making valuable shapes. Remember to tell the banker of any price changes. This example has parallels for countries that find their own technology outdated by changed circumstances.

D. Increasing the supply of raw materials or technology

From your own secret supply of extra paper you can "feed" an extra supply to one of the groups and announce to the world (i.e. all the groups) that a new deposit of raw materials has been discovered in this group. If this is done late in the game when everyone is running short of paper, it will quickly change relationships between groups. Parallels of this change in the real world include a new oil find or the discovery of mineral deposits.

E. Using the coloured sticky paper

Two groups will have a sheet of coloured sticky paper. They are not told anything about it and may not even notice that they have it; its real life parallel is a resource of which a country does not realise the full value. You can give it a value by secretly telling two other groups (by discreet written messages) that if they stick small squares of the paper to their products they will be worth four times the original value. (Tell the banker.) These groups will then start to search for the sticky paper. As the holders don't know its value they may well sell it cheaply and the first group will make a profit. Alternatively they might hold on to their resource until the end of the game and never let it be used, in which case its potential is never realised.

A parallel with the real world can be found in the history of Zambia. In the late nineteenth century Rhodes conducted negotiations with the local leaders for the exploitation and export of the copper deposits. Although copper had been used on a small scale for centuries in East Africa, few people envisaged the scale of the mining operation that Rhodes soon embarked upon. So the negotiations were very favourable to the British companies who went on benefiting until Zambia regained her independence in 1964. Today, Zambia owns a 51% controlling interest in her own copper mines.

Chile is another country where the copper has been mined at vast profit to multinational companies rather than the Chilean. In 1969, the mining investments in Chile of the Anaconda Mining Companv represented only 17% of the company's world wide investment, but in that year Chilean copper provided 80% of the company's world wide profits.

F. Some Possible Changes in the Game

Aid

During the game you could encourage one or two groups by granting them UN aid on certain conditions, for example, that a third of the goods produced with the aid should be paid back to the UN as interest. The aid could be given in the form of technology (e.g. extra scissors to one group for a short term only). Look out for examples of richer groups offering aid to poorer groups: what were the terms of the deal? In fact this is unlikely to happen unless the leader encourages it. Groups tend to be very reluctant to help others! Your observations and actions on aid can lead to discussion on the motives for aid giving in the real world. You can point out that Britain's aid programme in 1980-81 was £779 million, but that a lot of this was to be spent on goods and services in Britain.

Trade Associations

Trade associations develop during the game. Two or more groups may agree to cooperate for their mutual benefit. We are familiar with this kind of cooperation in the European Economic Community. Trade associations also exist in other parts of the world, in West Africa, Central America and Latin America, and, in East and Southern Africa, the PTA.

Tariffs and Duties

Some groups may place restrictions or charges on trading with other groups. Nations have tariff and quota arrangements which they have developed to protect their own interests. For example, in 1980 the following quotas and tariffs were operated by the EEC.

		Duty above
Quota for entry into EEC in tonnes of:		quota
Tinned Pineapple Chunks	45,000	23%
Instant Coffee	24,875	18%

Textile quotas are another example: in 1977, Britain reduced its imports of Indian hand loom shirts from 7.6 million pieces to 5.4 million peces to protect the UK textile industry.

Colonialisation and Annexation

These are other options which groups might try. A powerful group offers "protection" to another group or offers to absorb it, promising that its rights and assets will be respected. History is full of examples of annexation and colonisation: the growth of the British Empire in Africa and India will provide some good examples.

Producer Cartels

The groups with the most paper might join and decide to stabilise the price of paper to protect them from being individually exploited by the Grade A (industrialised) groups. Examples of cartels in the real world include O.P.E.C. (for the oil exporting countries), U.B.E.C. (Union of

110

Banana Exporting Countries) and I.B.A. (The International Bauxite Association). However, most producer cartels have not been particularly successful: O.P.E.C. remains the exception to the rule.

Trade Embargo

Groups with large supplies of paper could stop trading or reduce their amount of trade. By withholding supplies of paper, they may be able to improve the terms of trade for themselves and conserve stocks for the future. However, this would be risky without the protection of a cartel (see above). In recent years the oil-producing states of the Middle East have reduced production in order to conserve supplies while they diversify their economies.

Civil Strife and Industrial Unrest

The game leader can halt production by declaring a temporary general strike. He should remove the scissors from a Grade A group for a few minutes so that production has to stop. This situation may have parallels with civil and industrial disruptions caused by major strikes in industrial countries, for example, the General Strike in Britain in 1926.

These developments will probably not happen unless the leader introduces them. It is not necessary to try all of them within the game, but they are all situations which might well develop and they provoke discussion at the end of the game. One of the advantages of this game is that it is very open-ended: all kinds of alliances will emerge and then be broken and inevitably one of the players will ask you whether he or she can "cheat". Here we move into the morality of international trade: when is a bargain a bargain - and when is it exploitation?

Some guidelines for discussion

If the game goes according to plan, then it should soon become pretty clear to some of the groups of players that the whole set-up of the game is unbalanced right from the start. The groups aren't equal in resources, and complaints of "it's not fair" should soon start to reach the leader.

When the game is over and things have begun to quieten down, it will need patient steering on the leader's part to guide the de-briefing. The feeling of unfairness that will undoubtedly have been aroused in some of the groups ought to provide a useful jumping-off point for discussion.

The first hurdle for the discussion leader is to try to make the groups see that the game isn't "just a game", but a sort of "acted parable" that tries to reflect structures in the real world. If the players are aware that the game isn't fair, then it ought to be possible to get them to discuss why it isn't fair (for example, by getting them to look at how the resources and tools were distributed at the start).

You can then go on to look at the injustices in the structures of the world's trade and begin to appreciate the difficulties of arriving at a just system of exchange between the resource-owners and the tool-owners. The players' own experiences of helplessness, anger and potential violence during the course of the game could well be explored at this point, since they illustrate the sentiments felt on a world-wide scale by many of the Third World nations in the face of Western controlling interests. It might be useful to bring in some of the examples of exploitation at this stage (see above). How does an Indian tea-worker feel, for instance, when the decisions affecting his livelihood are made mainly by Western commercial interests?

Once this first hurdle has been cleared, then the next stage will be to dig a little deeper and try to explore more profound issues. If some groups of players felt that it was unreasonable for other groups to control all the tools, then the discussion could move on to concentrate on the questions of ownership and control. This is a difficult area of debate, so don't expect any easy answers! But the question "Who owns the world's resources?" ought to be asked, together with its counterpart "What right have nation-states to declare resources to be their 'property'?" If the leader can bring the discussion this far, then the debate will have moved from thinking about what is towards thinking about the way the world ought to be. Once the players have begun to ask questions about who has the right to dictate terms to the rest, it shouldn't be too hard to help them see that the fundamental issue is one of our own moral attitudes towards our wealth. If the world is an unfair place, and if we admit that its structures need changing, what sort of attitude should we have towards the world's resources and the use we make of them?

Acknowledgement: Christian Aid, London

113

Imports (B)

Ask students, singly or in small groups, to visit a local shop, and examine all the goods on a single shelf (probably, you would insist that the shop should not be mainly a food shop). Have students find out what goods are for sale, where they come from, what resources are needed to make them, where the resources probably came from, and if the goods are imported, what would be required to make the same good (or a substitute item) locally. Discuss the students' findings.

Balance of Trade (A) (134-137)

Make sure students understand the concept of a negative balance of trade.

Discuss:

a) the impact of a negative balance of trade on the country's debt;
b) the impact of a negative balance of trade on local people;
c) the effect of inflation on the balance of trade, and
d) ways in which the balance of trade might be improved, such as self-reliance, export diversification, and reduction of imports.

Make sure students understand the meaning of "foreign exchange" and "hard currency".

Balance of Trade (B)

Show students your country's balance of trade for the past few years. Discuss with them:

a) surpluses and deficits in balance of trade;
b) the nature of exports (primary, manufactured goods);
c) the nature of imports;
d) the effect of changing prices for primary goods; and
e) the effect of worldwide inflation

International Debt

Discuss the following issues with your students

1.   Your country's debt: what was money borrowed for? from whom? on what terms?
        Is the borrowed money used in ways that are likely to increase productivity?
3.   Was the money used to provide social services?
4.   Could the money have been used in other, more productive ways?

Foreign Investment (A) (137-142)

If there is a foreign company in your area, invite a representative to talk to your class. Before he comes, ask students to draw up a list of questions to ask during the discussion. You might include questions such as those listed below.

1. Where did the company originally get its capital?
2. Why did it decide to invest in your community?
3. What kind of goods does it produce, and where are the goods sold?
4. What policies does it have for training local personnel?
5. What foreign technical personnel does it bring in?
6. How does it contribute to your community's development?

Foreign Investment (B)

Discuss with students your country's policies towards foreign investors. Are there policies to attract foreign investment? Are there rules to control investment? How might those policies be changed? How could controls be enforced

Foreign Investment (C)

DEBATE: "FOREIGN INVESTMENT CAN HELP THE COUNTRY
DEVELOP BY BRINGING IN NEEDED CAPITAL"

Pro

- Most developing countries lack capital and skills to exploit resources.
- Foreign investment can help build industries which provide jobs and training.
- Foreign investment can diversify production and exports.

Con

- Foreign investors take away more in profits than they bring in capital.
- Foreign companies tend to pay low wages and exploit local resources.
- Foreign companies are likely to produce mostly primary products rather than diversifying.

NEW INTERNATIONAL ECONOMIC ORDER
(N.I.E.O.) - Role Play

U.N.C.T.A.D debate on the new international economic order. You may want to assign a small group to each part, as they involve quite difficult concepts.

Roles

REPRESENTATIVE FROM THE GROUP OF 77. This person argues that the North-South division reinforces Third World poverty, and that a more equitable distribution of the world's wealth will only come with a restructuring of the world trade system. He or she suggests that countries must agree to set up a more workable version of the Common Fund, so that countries which rely on the export of primary products will be able to get steadier and fairer prices. He or she might also suggest that world prices for primary products should be somehow linked to prices for manufactured goods. He or she should also demand that industrialised countries reduce tariffs and other protectionist measures that make it difficult for developing countries to sell manufactured goods to the industrialised "North".

Make sure students acting this part understand what the Group of 77 is, the Common Fund, STABEX, the generalised system of preferences, protectionism, and export diversification.

REPRESENTATIVE FROM LTHE UNITED STATES. This representative argues that industrialised countries are "of course" willing to accept a new international economic order, but the "South" must also accept that industrialised countries also have to recognise the needs of their electorates. Governments in the "North" must try to accommodate demands that competition from foreign countries' industries be reduced; he/she should refer to the problem of unemployment in capitalist industrialised countries, and explain that people fear that increased imports from developing countries will reduce job opportunities still further. He or she should also point out that many industrialised countries offer aid to developing countries, as part of an attempt to help them develop.

REPRESENTATIVE FROM JAMAICA. This person points out that in fact, competition from developing countries' industries does not reduce jobs in the "North" nearly as much as automation and new technology. He or she suggests that protectionism is therefore based on a myth, and will not achieve anything except greater poverty for the Third World. The representative should also point out the power relations involved in international negotiations: Third World countries can call for a New International Economic Order, but they have no way of insisting on it. (See the box on p. 145). He or she should point out that it is in the interest of industrialised countries to retain the current pattern of world trade, which benefits countries producing industrial goods more than it benefits producers of primary products.

REPRESENTATIVE FROM NIGERIA. This person argues that only producer cartels like O.P.E.C. (of which Nigeria is a member) will give exporters of primary products enough power to insist on changes in the structure of world trade. The representative describes O.P.E.C.'s successes in uniting oil producers, and forming a coalition that refuses to sell oil for less than the agreed-upon price. He or she calls on producers of other primary products to follow O.P.E.C's example.

REPRESENTATIVE FROM BRAZIL. This representative discusses problems with producer cartels, mentioning the failure of coffee producers to unite and demand a single price. (In the mid-70s, Brazil and other coffee-producing and exporting countries tried to set up such a cartel.) He/she points out some of the differences between petroleum and other primary products, such as:

a) world demand for oil is quite inelastic (does not change much when prices go up - or down) compared to demand for other products;
b) there are no substitutes for oil in most industrial processes, while most primary products can be replaced by man-made substitutes;
c) oil is found in only a few areas, while most primary products are found in many different countries, which can make unity harder; and
d) producers of agricultural products face the risk of a spoiled and wasted harvest if they try to withhold their product from the world market in order to force prices up.

REPRESENTATIVE FROM TANZANIA. Responding in particular to the United States' reference to aid, he or she calls for self-reliance as the best strategy for poor countries. The representative points out that most countries that rely on primary product export must ask foreign investors to run production (for example, mineral extraction in Southern Africa is largely controlled by the giant South African company Anglo-American). He or she argues that if developing countries rely on aid, loans, and foreign investment, they will go further into debt, and thus give the industrialised "North" great control over the development strategies of the poorer countries.

REPRESENTATIVE FOM THE SOVIET UNION. This representative argues that countries cannot rely on international change to restructure their exports and change the patterns of international trade. Instead, they must try to plan their economic growth - as the USSR does - to diversify their exports and increase productivity. He or she suggests that relying on private and foreign investment will not help poor countries develop industries and new productive capacity, because such investment is likely to continue old colonial patterns of production and trade.

Instructions

Try to get students to develop these arguments as far as possible. You may want to give them time before the role play to discuss each position in small groups, to make sure they understand what each position means, and why different countries are supposed to hold them. Make sure students understand the various concepts thoroughly, and can see how they are related to each other.

Chapter 7: Strategies for Development

Case Studies (197-220)

While teaching this section of the syllabus, and when looking at strategies for development in the abstract, it might prove helpful if students have different cases to refer to. Therefore, it might be worthwhile to divide the class into groups, and have each group read about one of the case study options and perhaps do further research on that country. Then in discussions of abstract strategy options, ask students from each group to report on how "their" country has dealt with a particular question. This may help to ground the discussion in reality, and to show students that different countries have answered similar questions in very different ways.

Defining Development (151-156)

Make sure students understand the difference between the three basic definitions of development. Discuss with them:

a) how your country defines development (look at the goals listed in the development plan, if there is one), and
b) other ways a government might choose to define development

Indicators of "Development"

Having discussed how your government seems to define development, look at different indicators in your country and see whether they show any improvement in people's standard of living. Look at changes in the GNP (economic growth rate) for the past few years. Look at changes in indicators of quality of life such as literacy rates, mortality rates and infant mortality.

Have students, singly or in small groups, design posters and diagrams to illustrate graphically what these rates mean. For example, if they choose literacy rates, they might show that seven out of ten people in your country have learned to read. If students choose different indicators, you may want to post their charts in the classroom so they can learn from each others' work.

Problems of Statistical Evaluation

Divide the students into pairs. Have students interview each other about:

a) what they have produced in the last month - what goods of value;
b) what goods they have bought, and the value, and
c) what services they have received, and the value of those services.

Students should realise quickly how difficult it can be to determine the GNP, as they see how hard it is for statisticians to find accurate information. Discuss the problems of information-gathering with the class, and see if they have any suggestions for improving data.

Make sure students understand how important data-collection can be if the government wants to plan development carefully.

Industrial Growth (156-160)

Discuss with students your country's policies toward industrialisation. You might want to look at the following issues:

1. Infrastructure: where are new roads and railroads put in? Who decides? Who pays for new infrastructure?
2. Industrial growth: what system has the government got for raising capital (foreign investment, parastatal companies, a mixture of state and private owned investment)? What kinds of incentives are offered to get people to produce specific kinds of goods? What goods are these, and why does the government want to promote those kinds of production?
3. Decentralisation: what efforts, if any, has the government made to decentralise industrial growth? Why might such efforts be needed? What success have these efforts had?

Decentralisation

After students have read the box (p 159) on China's decentralisation policies, discuss with them:

a) the possible advantages of decentralising industrial expansion;
b) the possible disadvantages of decentralising; and
c) the possibilities of decentralising industrial growth in your country

(remember, if there are already concentrated industrial centres, it may be difficult to change that pattern quickly).

Remember to ask students how "their" case study has dealt with this question.

Small-Scale Industries

Discuss with students your country's policy toward promoting small-scale industries. Some points to consider include:

a) capital requirements for small industries;
b) skills requirements for small-scale industries;
c) problems of marketing and competition (if everyone chooses to produce the same goods, what will be the result?);
d) problems of diversification (how will an emphasis on small-scale industry affect your country's ability to change its position in international trade?); and
e) what kind of "mix" can be found of small- and large-scale industry?

Rural Development (165-168)

Discuss with students the many different aspects of rural development that must go together. Some points to consider include:

a) providing economic assistance to rural peasants (problems of remoteness, lack of capital,etc.);

b) lack of skills and knowledge needed for improving productivity (how can this be overcome?); and

c) problems of distribution of resources (how might this affect peasants' productivity?).

Women's Special Needs (155, box)

Discuss women's special needs with the class. Some points to raise are listed below.

1. How child care and domestic work can interfere with women's ability to make good incomes.

2. Why women end up responsible for most child care and domestic work.

3. What policy your government has designed to help women deal with their "double day" of domestic and productive work. (Some aspects to look at are the provision of maternity benefits and the provision of day care and creches.)

4. What changes have there been in how people view women's work and their abilities? What opportunities are open or closed to women? Why?

Land Reform (167-168)

Discuss with students:

(a) your country's land reform policy (if any);
(b) projects in land reform undertaken; and
(c) progress made in changing the pattern of rural land ownership.

Rural Development (B)

DEBATE: "INDUSTRIAL GROWTH SHOULD BE SEEN AS THE MAIN BASIS FOR ECONOMIC GROWTH"

Pro

- Provides new jobs.
- Reduces the need for importing manufactured goods.
- Raises the productivity of each hour of labour.

Con

- People live in rural areas, and their productivity should be increased in the fields where they already work.
- Food self-sufficiency is an important step in reducing the country's dependence.

- If agricultural productivity is improved first, a surplus can later be invested in industrial growth.

A MILLION MALOTI FOR RURAL DEVELOPMENT? - Role Play

The Setting

Two villages are located in the foothill region of Lesotho. They are Ha Ramanganga and Ntlafatsong.

Ha Ramanganga

It has a population of 50 people. It lies high up on the shoulder of the mountain, with a rough path going down to the valley below. There are a few small terraced fields, where the villagers grow crops. Some of them own some cattle, or sheep and goats, that graze on the mountain pastures.

There are no modern facilities at all. Very few children have been to school. Women fetch water from a spring a kilometre down the hillside. Many babies are malnourished, for the people cannot grow quite enough food, and they have few ways of earning money. Some men go to work in the mines. Others sell the wool and mohair from their flocks.

Ntlafatsong

It has a population of 200 people. It lies down in the valley below the mountain, on sloping land near a small river. There is a bad gravel road which goes to the town 50 km. away. After heavy rain, even trucks cannot get through to Ntlafatsong. There are fields, but many are badly eroded. Nearby pastures are over-grazed.

There is an old, two-roomed school that goes up to Std. 4. A cafe exists but has only a few goods to sell, and they are so expensive that people cannot always afford them. Water is fetched from the river, but it is polluted, and people often get sick. Recently a woman was chosen to go and train as a Village Health Worker, but the nearest clinic is in the town.

The Problem

The government has received a grant of M. 1,000.000 (one million maloti) to spend on rural development. The donors have asked that it be used to improve one small area, preferably just one village. They said the government should find an area where the people are very poor and in great need.

A survey of villages was undertaken, and it was found that these two villages are amongst the poorest in the country. The government would like to concentrate all the improvements on Ntlafatsong, and resettle all the people from Ha Ramanganga in the valley. Their reasons are:

- the donors suggest the money be spent on improving one village completely;
- it will cost double the amount if they have to build two schools, two clinics, and so on, and
- it would be expensive to build a road to Ha Ramanganga.

The government says, however, that the people of the two villages should make the decisions about what improvements they need in their lives. They should also decide whether to remain as two villages, or to join together as one. (The two villages are 6 km. apart.)

The Pitso

A government official from the Ministry of Co-operatives and Rural Development comes to the village of Ntlafatsong. The chief calls a pitso and invites the villagers of Ha Ramangaga to join them.

What they say - Media Reports

RADIO LESOTHO

"Friends of the Lesotho Government have donated a sum of a million maloti to Lesotho. It is not yet clear where and how the money will be spent. The sum is, however, earmarked for rural improvements. One of the two villages, Ntlafatsong and Ha Ramanganga, is a possible choice. Obviously roads, water supplies and clinics are likely improvements."

"MOLETSI OA BASOTHO" (10.06.83)

MINISTER SPEAKS

In his address to a pitso at Mafika-mahlo, the Minister of Rural Development, the Honourable Morena Sekama, disclosed that the sum of M.1,000,000 has been given to the government of Lesotho to be spent on rural improvement. Two villages are already chosen as beneficiaries. The donors will periodically visit the country to evaluate progress.

"LESELINYANA LA LESOTHO" (14.06.83) (Editorial)

Rural improvement is a very important undertaking for developing countries, Lesotho included. After reading the article in *Moeletsi oa Basotho (10.06.83) "Minister Speaks"*, one hopes that the said sum will be spent on genuinely poor villages, whose selection will be based on real needs, not political affiliation. Rumour has it that the government wants one of the villages to be resettled. In that case, will there be any compensation? Who will help the villagers build new houses? The government must not disturb people's lives without paying them compensation.

"MOCHOCHONONO" (1.07.83)

The government of Lesotho, in its dedication to improvements of the living standards of rural people, has again managed to secure a grant of M1,000,000 from its friends to spend on rural development.

A survey conducted to identify rural needs has shown two villages that qualify for the grant. These are Ha Ramanganga and Ntlafatsong. Necessary steps are being taken to involve the inhabitants of these villages in decision-making.

HAND-WRITTEN PAPERS, SCATTERED IN THE VILLAGE

IS IT TRUE
- that Ha Ramanganga must move?
- that new houses and fields will be given to the resettled villagers?
- that the government has got enough money to build these houses?
- that Ha Ramanganga is being moved because it opposes the government?
- that the plans are already decided and made?
- that Ha Ramanganga people will have to live under the chief of Ntlafatsong?
WE SHALL NOT BE MOVED! - IT IS NOT TRUE!

Guidelines for Roles

GOVERNMENT OFFICIAL from the Ministry of Co-operatives and Rural Development (Make up a speech from these notes.)

- There is a grant of one million maloti, to be spent on a very poor village.
- The survey showed that Ha Ramanganga and Ntlafatsong are both very poor.
- It would be much cheaper to improve one village, and resettle the people from the other village at the improved one.
- The government wishes people to make their own decisions.
- The people of Ha Ramanganga and Ntlafatsong have been called to the pitso to discuss which village should improved.
- The people should tell the government what to spend the money on.

CHIEF OF NTLAFATSONG (Make up a speech from these notes.)

- Thanks to the government official.
- It is obvious that Ntlafatsong should be chosen as the improved village.
- The ground is much flatter, there is a large population, a school already exists. It is closer to the main road.
-The improvements needed are:1) a better road to the town;
 2) a clean, piped water supply, and
 3) a clinic.

- The people of Ha Ramanganga should move down to Ntlafatsong and settle there.

CHIEF RAMANGANGA   (Make up a speech from these notes)

- He does not agree with the Chief of Ntlafatsong.
- Why was the pitso called at Ntlafatsong and not at Ha Ramanganga?
- This shows the government has a bias against Ha Ramanganga.
- He and his people love their village and do not want to move.
- Their life is satisfactory, a few improvements will do.
- He cannot work under the Chief of Ntlafatsong

AN OLD MAN FROM HA RAMANGANGA (Join the discussion from time to time along these lines.)

- He supports his chief.
- There are no problems in Ha Ramanganga and no improvements are needed.
- Resettlement will anger the gods.
- They cannot leave the graves of their fathers, nor their fathers' fields.

SHOPKEEPER (Argues strongly from time to time from the following point of view.)

- He has a cafe in Ntlafatsong.
- An improved road to the village would make it much easier to bring in supplies, and the cost of transport would be less, so goods would be cheaper.
- He would have more business if the people from Ha Ramanganga settled in the valley. At present they seldom come to his shop.
- The people of Ha Ramanganga would have a better life in the valley; they could buy all the good things from his cafe.
- If a clinic was built, he would get customers from other villages too, as they would come to the clinic, and stop at his cafe on the way.

PRIEST (He tries to persuade the villagers that Ntlafatsong only should be improved.)

- The church at Ntlafatsong is very small, just an old rondavel.
- He tries to go to Ha Ramanganga to hold services, but he is old, and the path is steep.
- If Ha Ramanganga moves down, he will have a bigger congregation and they can build a new church and a new house for him.

MINER FROM HA RAMANGANGA (He is used to the town life of Johannesburg and finds Ha Ramanganga very backward, so he wants his people to move. He uses arguments such as the following)

- It is difficult to transport baggage and modern goods up the path to his house at Ha Ramanganga.
- He attended school up to Std 7, and knows how important health and hygiene are.
- As far as graves of grandparents are concerned, he says "dead men don't bite".

TRADITIONAL HEALER (He is very worried that his patients will all go to the new clinic, so he tries hard to persuade people to leave Ha Ramanganga alone.)

- A clinic is unnecessary, as he can cure illness.
- The way of life in Ha Ramanganga is a good way; young people respect their elders and people are happy.
- If the villagers move, the gods will be angry; drought, thunderstorm and ill-health will result.

VILLAGE HEALTH WORKER FROM NTLAFATSONG (She is very proud of her new training, and wants a proper clinic in Ntlafatsong.)

- She has modern drugs to cure illness which work better than the traditional ones.
- If the money is split between the villages, there will only be a small clinic in each. But if there is one village, the clinic can be big, and a proper nurse can be employed.
- The river water is dirty and they must have a piped supply from a clean spring.

-Children must be taught hygiene in school, and all children must go to school.

COMMITTEE WOMAN FROM NTLAFATSONG (She is pro-government, and does not want the opposition supporters in Ha Ramanganga to come down. She tries to frighten them.)

- The government has no money, so it won't keep its promise to rebuild the houses for the people of Ha Ramanganga
- Why should the government help these people anyway, they never supported the government?
- Let Ha Ramanganga stay where it is.
- A little of the money should be spent on a school for Ha Ramanganga and to improve the path up the mountain.

WOMAN FROM HA RAMANGANGA (She is anti-government. She does not want to move, but says that the government is being unfair if it gives all the money to one village. She asks the man from the Ministry to split the grant.)

- Why should Ha Ramanganga have to move just to get improvements?
- The government should give half the money to each village.
- The people of Ha Ramanganga need a school, a small clinic, and a pumped water supply so the women don't have to fetch water from so far.
- A road must be built to Ha Ramanganga.

MAN FROM HA RAMANGANGA (He wants to know where his cattle will graze if he moves down to the valley.)

- He has many cattle and small stock.
- The pastures in the valley are overgrazed, so he wishes to keep his animals on the mountain.
- Some of the money should be used to build a veterinary post in Ha Ramanganga and train a local man as a vet, to cure animal diseases.
- Why is the government only interested in maize? Why doesn't it help stock-farmers?

TEACHER FROM NTLAFATSONG (He tries to persuade the meeting to think of the children.)

-There is already a school at Ntlafatsong, which can be easily enlarged.
- Children do not come down from Ha Ramanganga because it is so far to walk.
- The money should be used to build a small school at Ha Ramanganga for Stds. 1-4.
- The school at Ntlafatsong should be enlarged to take the higher standards.
- The villages should remain where they are and each should receive some help.

WOMAN FROM HA RAMANGANGA (She listens carefully to everyone, and tries to give a sensible viewpoint.)

- Ha Ramanganga is a nice village, but life is hard there for the women.
- They have to fetch water from far away, and there is little fuel.
- Life would be easier in Ntlafatsong.
- On the other hand, she is afraid of going to live among strangers.
- She suggests the women of the two villages should have a meeting to see how they can help each other.

OLD MAN FROM NTLAFATSONG (He acts as a peace-maker when quarrels break out.)

- In the past the villages have taken different sides.
- Now it is time to come together to work in peace.
- The people of Ntlafatsong should welcome the people from Ha Ramanganga and give them sites for houses, fields, and help them build new homes.
- Moshoeshoe built a nation out of different tribes; can they not build a new community out of two different villages?

Suggestions for Playing

(Teachers should feel free to change and adapt as they think fit.)

Preparation

Teacher explains the "setting". The sheet on WHAT THEY SAY could also be circulated, or students coukd write up the extracts on large shets of newsprint for display on the classroom wall.

Allocation of roles

Roles are given out and allocated to students by agreement. Time should be allowed for students to discuss their own and other people's roles so they know who their fellow-characters are. They should be aware who belongs to "their" village, who shares or opposes their views, etc. More roles can be invented in the same way, so as to involve all the class. For example:
- chief's wife, wives and husbands of other characters;
- man who wants to start a taxi-service from Ntlafatsong to the town;
- son of the traditional healer, who wants to be a doctor (sons and daughters of other characters;)
- agricultural extension officer;
- deserted wife of a migrant labourer;
- a sick person, and
- a very old woman etc.

It is important that the students think about each role, and try to imagine the character they are playing. Encourage all to join fully in the discussion at the pitso. Explain that the guidelines are just to give the starting point; it is up to each student to "develop his or her role".

Space

The classroom furniture is suitably arranged for the "pitso", or the class moves to a hall, or outside.

134

Chairperson

Should the teacher chair the "pitso"?

Pro

- the teacher can steer the discussion in a constructive direction;
- the teacher can prevent emotions from getting too high, and
- the teacher can encourage all to speak.

Con

- students may talk more freely if teacher does not take part;
- students need experience of chairmanship, and
- the teacher can observe, and make notes, so that she or he can remind the class afterwards exactly what happened.

Time

It can take a single period, a double period, or several separate lessons.

Process

What actually takes place depends very much on how the students play their roles. The more experienced the students are in role-playing, the more they will be able to develop their arguments and creates a "real" situation. It is possible that fierce arguments will arise between the villagers. It is possible that agreement is quickly reached. The teacher must decide at what point to stop.

Variations

Separate pitsos could be held by each village before the joint one. If no decision is easily reached, the meeting could be adjourned to another "day" (another lesson).

Debriefing

Plenty of time - at least one period and perhaps more - must be given for reflection and analysis.

1. Reflection

What happened? Did the villages co-operate or argue? What kinds of development did they want the government to provide?

2. Analysis

Compare the situation with reality. How true to life was the simulation? Do chiefs, villagers and government officials really behave like that? Was the outcome positive or negative? What could make such a discussion constructive in real life?

3. Learning

What have we learnt about development in Lesotho from this simulation?

4. Consolidation

Students can write up some kind of report - individually or in small groups - summing up what they have learnt. This could take several forms, depending on the students' level. For example:
- a simple report of the simulation;
- the report the government official gave his Ministry;
- the development plan the villagers drew up;
- the project proposal the government sent to the donors, or
- "What our Village Needs," "Problems in Rural Development," etc.

Replay

After reflection and analysis, the game could be played again, perhaps with an agreement among the players to try to reach a really constructive solution.

Place in the Scheme of Work

This can be played as an "opener" for the topic "Rural Development" (Section 8, J.C. syllabus) or as consolidation, or even evaluation, at the end of the topic.

The situation could also be taken purely as a "case-study". Here the students read about the situation and discuss it. They then suggest solutions, individually or in groups, for the problems of the two villages. There is no need to act out the roles. On the other hand, acting will help them to remember the stories, and through acting attitudes may be changed. It is also most enjoyable and therefore motivating.

Objectives that may be achieved

Knowledge: Students will list a number of rural improvements and describe what benefits each will bring to the community. They will list a number of reasons why people oppose change, and explain the economic reasons for moving two villages into one.

Concepts: Students will understand and correctly use terms such as: rural development; social change; traditionalism; conflict; aid, and donor.

Skills: Students will practise presenting reasoned arguments, evaluating opposing arguments, writing a report, drawing up a development project.

Attitudes: Through acting roles, students may come to have deeper understanding of, and sympathy for, the views and feelings of others Through simulated discussion, agreement and decision-making, they may come to prize cooperation and tolerance above conflict and suspicion.

Acknowledgement: Mrs Rosaliah Ramoholi, *Lesotho Development Studies Ideas Book,* 1983.

Appropriate Technology (157, box; 168-172)

Ask students if they can think of any examples of "inappropriate" technology, where machines seemed to waste local resources or to be so complex they could not be easily repaired.

Ask them for examples of "appropriate" technology; discuss how these examples are inexpensive, easy to maintain and repair, but increase productivity. Discuss with students some of the problems with appropriate technology: why do people sometimes resist buying intermediate or appropriate technology? What do they prefer? Why? Is this a problem, or is it the way things should be?

FIELD TRIPS

A. If there is an "appropriate" or "renewable energy" technology centre near your school, take students to see some of the inventions. When they return, ask students to write essays addressing the following kinds of issues:

(a) what they saw;
(b) how it was made;
(c) how much it cost to make;
(d) how useful it might be;
(e) how widely it has been accepted;
(f) what steps have been made to make the invention available to people; and
(g) whether students feel it is a useful and worthwhile project.

B. If there are any parastatal projects - either industrial or agricultural - near you, take students. Before you go, have students draw up lists of questions, such as those listed below.

1. What is produced? What is it used for?
2. Why did the government nationalise this project
3. What problems have the parastatal's managers had in:
- providing services and/or goods to the community;
- finding raw materials, skills;
- distributing goods and services, and
- keeping costs low.

4. Do the workers at the parastatal view their jobs differently from people in the private sector?

5. What suggestions can students make for organising the production differently?

Chapter 8: Development in Southern Africa

South Africa (175-180)

Make sure students understand what apartheid is, and how it works. Discuss with them its impact on your country; ask if they know of any examples of its impact. For example, what did they learn from their interviews of returned migrant labourers? What impact has it had in terms of racial prejudices in your country? What impact has it had on your country's population size?

South Africa - Economic Ties

Look at a map of railroads and roads in your country. How does your country's infrastructure link into South Africa? What impact might this have?

Discuss how your country relies on South Africa's ports and industries, and on its markets. What goods are imported through South Africa? What goods are imported from South Africa?

What economic arrangements exist between your country and South Africa (Customs Union, Preferential Trade Agreements)? What impact do these ties have on your country, if any? Do they limit the choices open to your government?

South Africa's Development Strategy (181-183)

Make sure students understand the different aspects of South Africa's developoment strategies in the 20th century, including:

a)   government control over labour supply, through pass laws and labour bureaux;
b)   parastal companies supplying crucial ingredients for industrial growth;
c)   import-substitution policies protecting local industry; and

d)   job protection/job reservation clauses protecting white workers' jobs.

Make sure you discuss the importance of gold in the world economy.

Current Affairs

Throughout the year, you may want to keep a bulletin board of newspaper clippings of articles about the region, with special sections for SADCC, economic and military destabilisation, change inside South Africa, ties between South Africa and your country and efforts by the Front-Line States to help find a solution to problems in the region.

Namibia

If possible, invite a SWAPO official to visit your class to discuss the reasons for, and the history of the liberation struggle. If this is not possible, have students singly or in groups research some aspect of the Namibian struggle, and report back to the class. Some areas for research might include:

a) history of German rule in Namibia;
b) South African rule in Namibia;
c) SWAPO's policies and plans for the future;
d) the history of the war in Namibia (and Angola); and
e) the attempts to end the wars, including the role of the Frontline States, up to the emergence of independent Namibia in March, 1990.

Destabilisation

Using your current affairs bulletin as a resource, discuss with students the reasons for and the effects of South Africa's destabilisation policy. What impact has this policy had on your country? What can your country do to defend itself? What has it done? Have students design posters about destabilisation.

Refugee Policy

One of the problems facing countries in southern Africa is what they should do about refugees from South Africa and from SA-sponsored wars, e.g. in Mozambique and Angola . Discuss why people flee South Africa, why many countries in the region are worried about the presence of refugees, and why the United Nations has said it is every country's moral duty to give refugees asylum. Then look at:

a) your country's policy toward refugees - and toward support for the liberation movements, and
b) how the refugee policy is implemented (what steps a refugee must go through to get asylum, etc.)

You might try to invite an official from the ministry in your country which deals with refugees or from the United Nations High Commission for Refugees to discuss the problem and possible solutions in your country.

Liberation Support (A)

DEBATE: "THE COUNTRIES BORDERING SOUTH AFRICA WILL HAVE TO ACCEPT SOME RESPONSIBLITY FOR THE LIBERATION STRUGGLE INSIDE SOUTH AFRICA"

Pro

- All countries should support the effort to remove apartheid.
- Destabilisation means no countries in the region are safe until the apartheid regime is removed.
- Most countries in the region are economically tied to South Africa, and will not be themselves completely liberated until South Africa is free.

Con

- Apartheid is an internal affair.
- It is not safe to support the liberation movements.
- Independent countries in the region must solve their own problems first.

Liberation Support (B)

Ask students what they can do to help the liberation struggle, through distributing information in their community, helping refugees, donating funds or other activities.

ORGANISATION OF AFRICAN UNITY - Role Play

Assign each student (or pair of students) to represent a country in the O.A.U. Give students time to research about the country, and to figure out what that country's position might be on issues currently debated in the O.A.U. Students might look at magazines like *New Africa* to find out about "their" country, or write to the country's embassy in your country.

Hold an O.A.U. debate, with each student representing "their" country's concerns. You may want to focus on a few particular issues (tell students beforehand what these issues will be). Some issues for debate might include: "Liberation struggles in Southern Africa", and "The problems of refugees in the Horn of Africa".

Try to make the debate as real as possible. You might want to set up the classroom to look as much like an assembly as possible.

SADCC (A) (186-189)

Discuss with students the following questions.

1.   SADCC's aims and objectives - why are they important?
2.   What projects is SADCC creating for development in the region?
3.   What problems might the different governments face in working together?
4   What are the prospects for complete regional cooperation through SADCC?

SADCC (B)

Look at your country's role in SADCC, especially at the issues below.

1.   Which area of development planning is your country responsible for?
2   What projects are under way or in planning stages?
3.   Why were these projects chosen?
4   What progress has been made in your country's area of responsibility?

Films

There are many recent films about development around the world. If you write to your local UNDP office, or to your country's Ministry of Information, you may be able to get a list of films about development in Southern Africa or the liberation struggles, which you could borrow for free to show your class.

SADCC - Role Play

Before beginning this role play, divide students into groups, each representing one of the SADCC countries. Give students several days to find out about "their" countries' responsibilities in SADCC, what has been done so far, and what is planned for the future. Then hold a SADCC "summit meeting", where representatives from each country discuss what has been achieved, and what is hoped for in the future. Some general questions to debate at the summit (in addition to whatever has been discussed at the most recent summit) include:

a) the problems of relying on donor funds for SADCC projects;

b) the extent to which donor funds have arrived for SADCC projects, and alternative sources of funds;

c) the problems in cooperation (what if countries disagree about priorities?), and

d) the problems in coordinating negotiations with multinationals, and why it might be important.

SECTION IV

BACKGROUND MATERIAL FOR TEACHERS

There are many books on the history of Southern Africa, and on the theories behind different views of development. Of course we cannot list all of them here; we can only suggest a few basic books that might help you in discussions of some of the issues raised in the course. They are listed alphabetically, rather than by topic; however, we have mentioned books in the main part of the teachers' guide where they seemed particularly relevant.

Braudel, Fernand, *Capitalism and Material Life, 1400 -1800* Glasgow: William Collins Sons and Co., 1974. Looks at the changes and events leading to the Industrial Revolution in Europe.

Callinicos, Luli, *Gold and Workers: A People's History of South Africa, Vol. 1* Johannesburg: Ravan Press, 1980. A simple and clear discussion of the rise of the migrant labour system in Southern Africa; useful as a teaching aid, because it has illustrations and quotes that illustrate the main themes.

Centre for World Development *Education Resource Catalogue*, available from 128 Buckingham Palace Road, London SW1, U.K. Lists teaching aids for development studies, and how to get them, including games, films, posters, etc.

Davidson, Basil, *Africa in Modern History*. London: Allen Lane, 1978. Excellent simple history of Africa in the 20th century, with good illustrations.

E.D.A. People's Workbook. Available from E.D.A., P.O. Box 62054, Marshalltown 2107, Johannesburg. Gives good instructions for many practical activities in Southern Africa (especially useful for rural areas).

Also includes short comic history of imperialism in Southern Africa (available separately as *Vusi Goes Home*).

Development Studies Ideas Book. Rima: National University of Lesotho, 1983. Compiled from reports and suggestions of teachers in Lesotho, and edited by Janet Stuart. Suggests classroom activities and field trips for J.C. - Level students.

Harvey, Charles, *Papers on the Economy of Botswana.* London: Heinemann Educational Books, 1981. Collection of papers on specific, and quite technical aspects of Botswana's economy, suggesting different policy options.

Hanlon, Joseph, *Beggar Your Neighbours.* A study of South African destabilisation

Martin, David and Phyllis Johnson, *Destructive Engagement.* Harare: Zimbabwe Publishing House, 1986.

Martin, David and Phyllis Johnson, *The Struggle for Zimbabwe*, Harare: Zimbabwe Publishing House, 1981. Describes the struggle for independence.

Nsekela, Amon J. (ed.), *Southern Africa: Toward Economic Liberation.* London: Rex Collings, 1981. Papers presented at 1979 and 1980 SADCC meetings. Looks at economic dependence, regional integration, finance, agriculture, energy and resources, employment and trade patterns. Also provides some basic data about SADCC countries.

Parsons, Neil, *A New History of Southern Africa.* London: Macmillan Educational Books 1982. Excellent reference book for teachers in Southern Africa.

Rodney, Walter, *How Europe Underdeveloped Africa.* Reprinted in 1982 by Zimbabwe Publishing House, Box BW 350, Harare. Gives simple, clear discussion of the impact of slave trade and imperialism on the continent of Africa.

Seidman, Ann, *An Economics Textbook for Africa*. London: Methuen and Co., 1972. Clear introduction to many basic economic concepts, with African examples.

Stephen, David, *The San of the Kalahari*. London: Minority Rights Group Report No. 56, 1982. Short, simple discussion of the San, their history, culture and current problems.

Thompson, EP, *The Making of the English Working Class*. London: Penguin Books, 1963. Discusses the effect of the industrial revolution on the people of Britain.

www.ingramcontent.com/pod-product-compliance
Lightning Source LLC
Chambersburg PA
CBHW062037270326
41929CB00014B/2464